STUDIES IN

ANTHROPOLOGICAL METHOD

General Editors

GEORGE AND LOUISE SPINDLER
Stanford University

MANUAL FOR KINSHIP ANALYSIS

MANUAL FOR
KINSHIP ANALYSIS

Second Edition

ERNEST L. SCHUSKY

Southern Illinois University

HOLT, RINEHART AND WINSTON

New York   Chicago   San Francisco   Atlanta
Dallas   Montreal   Toronto   London   Sydney

FOREWORD

Anthropology has been, since the turn of the century, a significant influence shaping Western thought. It has brought into proper perspective the position of our culture as one of many, and has challenged universalistic and absolutistic assumptions and beliefs about the proper condition of man. Anthropology, the study of man, has been able to make this contribution mainly through its descriptive analyses of esoteric ways of life. Only in the last decades of anthropology's comparatively short existence as a science have anthropologists developed systematic theories about human behavior in its transcultural dimensions. Only still more recently have anthropological techniques of data collection and analysis become explicit and replicable.

Nearly every issue of every professional anthropological journal contains statements of methodological innovations. Our discipline is in a seminal period of development.

Teachers of anthropology have previously been handicapped by the lack of clear, authoritative statements of how anthropologists collect and analyze relevant data. The results of fieldwork are available to students in the ethnographer's published works. Although these demonstrate cultural diversity and integration, social control, religious behavior, marriage customs, and the like, clear, systematic statements about how the facts are gathered and interpreted are rare in the literature readily available to students. Without this information the alert "consumer" of anthropological results is left uninformed about the processes of our science—an unsatisfying state of affairs for both the student and the professor.

Our Studies in Anthropological Method series is designed to help relieve this tension. Each study in the series focuses on some manageable aspect of modern anthropological methodology. Each one demonstrates significant aspects of the processes of gathering, ordering, and interpreting data. The studies are written by professional anthropologists who have done fieldwork and who have made significant contributions to the science of man and his works. The authors explain how they go about this work, and to what end. We think the studies will be useful in courses ranging from the introductory to the graduate levels.

ABOUT THE AUTHOR

Ernest L. Schusky is Professor of Anthropology and Chairman of the Anthropology Faculty at Southern Illinois University, Edwardsville. His major interests are social structure, culture change, and applied anthropology. He completed his Ph.D. at the University of Chicago and has done fieldwork among the Papago and Dakota Indians. In the summer of 1964 he studied in India as a Fulbright scholar; in 1966–1967 he was a post-doctoral student at the London School of Economics. His monograph, *The Right To Be Indian*, has recently been reissued by the Indian Historian Press. In addition to contemporary political problems among Indians, Dr. Schusky has published on Dakota demography, religion, and economic development.

ABOUT THE BOOK

Given the peculiarities and attenuated simplicity of the American kinship system, the study of kinship, one of the subjects closest to the hearts of many anthropologists, has always been one of the most difficult for students to understand. Most instructors who have taught a beginning class have had the experience of trying to explain the kinship systems of other societies to bewildered students who do not understand their own, and whose ethnocentrism blocks their comprehension of others.

This manual is designed to make available to students at beginning and intermediate levels a comprehensible treatment of the subject. The previous manual, first published in 1965, has been very widely used. The present manual has retained the most useful features of the previous one and has updated coverage to include such new developments as componential analysis, new systems of notation and diagramming, as well as references to some of the most significant theory and relevant literature.

Dr. Schusky has given us a clear statement of the essential features of the study of kinship. He introduces concepts sequentially and demonstrates each major step of the analysis. He provides exercises that build understanding as the complexities unfold. Though he directs the attention of the user of this manual to basic essentials in the study of kinship, he also provides insight into some of the major conceptual problems of the study. The result will be useful, we think, to many students and instructors in general anthropology and intermediate social organization courses.

GEORGE AND LOUISE SPINDLER
General Editors

Landgut Burg, West Germany

CONTENTS

Introduction

ANTHROPOLOGISTS HAVE STUDIED kinship more than any other single topic. In these extensive studies involving complex kinship charts, symbols, and formulas, anthropologists may even seem to be performing mystic rituals rather than making an analysis of human behavior or cognition. Proportionally, anthropologists spend as much time analyzing kinship as sociologists spend with social classes. A major reason for this study is that both kinship and stratification exhibit much regular, recurrent behavior, and it is only on the basis of regular, repetitive phenomena that generalizations can be built and tested.

The regularities of kinship were recognized early in the history of anthropology. The first scholars found that many different peoples of the world classified relatives in much the same way and that there were several basic types of kinship terminologies. Although they concentrated on ordering these different types into evolutionary stages, even these first anthropologists realized that the complex status relations of a kinship system must be understood in relation to other areas, such as economic, political, psychological, and sexual behavior. Edward Tylor (1889) was one of the first to discover a number of such relationships which he termed "adhesions." Tylor soon saw that statistical tests would be necessary to determine the significance of an adhesion. Lewis H. Morgan (1877), who concentrated on the evolutionary stages of kinship, attempted to demonstrate that different marriage practices determined the various kinship systems that he had classified previously (1870). Group marriage, for instance, would mean that a child of the group would call many men his "father." Although Morgan overly stressed the importance of kinship terminology for reconstructing social evolutionary stages, he laid a sound foundation through his own observation and in his collection of questionnaires about kin terminologies from around the world (Fortes 1969; White 1957).

Morgan (1870) had based his collection of terminology upon a long questionnaire that yielded a limited sort of dictionary. W. H. R. Rivers (1914) improved ethnographic methodology by collecting lengthy genealogies, or actual kinship charts, from many individuals of a society. From his real genealogies Rivers constructed the ideal systems that Morgan had gathered, but in addition, Rivers saw practices not reflected by the ideal terminology alone. Furthermore, he found that most peoples enjoy talking about their relatives, past and present, so that the collection of genealogies gave the fieldworker a convenient entry into a society as well as providing data on the essential aspects of behavior.

While Rivers was discovering such a practical use for kinship study, other anthropologists continued to reconstruct history through the comparison of kinship systems. Similarities between kinship systems certainly do indicate the possibility

1

of a common origin for societies, but no way was ever found to reconstruct the past only by comparison of kinship systems. However, hypotheses yielded by such comparisons frequently suggested past associations that could be confirmed by other methods. A variety of systems among the Plains Indians, for instance, immediately suggests diverse origins for these peoples although much of their material culture and value systems are quite similar.

Although the social evolutionists and the early historicalists failed to reconstruct history through kinship, their effort has continued. Murdock (1949) suggests a logical sequence of change through several successive types of social structure, but his theory is still being tested. Neo-evolutionists hope to discover several courses of evolution that kinship systems may have taken. Elman Service (1962) argues that present classifications of kinship systems have been useless for formulating stages of development, but by combining kin statuses with statuses from other social systems, courses of evolution may be found. He suggests (1962:187) that simple stages have only kinship statuses while later stages may exhibit a similar kinship system but combine it with other status networks. At a minimum, the work should indicate to ethnohistorians and even archeologists that kinship studies are within their province.

Most work on kinship, however, has continued to be in the narrower realm of social or cultural anthropology. Modern studies date, more or less, from the American anthropologists, Alfred Kroeber and Robert Lowie, and from the British anthropologists, A. R. Radcliffe-Brown and Bronislaw Malinowski. Kroeber (1909) showed kinship to be more complex than indicated by Morgan. In opposition to Rivers, Kroeber stressed his view that terminology was primarily a linguistic phenomenon. He believed that kin behavior would best be understood in psychological, rather than sociological, terms. Radcliffe-Brown and Malinowski, on the other hand, continually saw kinship as a sociological institution. They stressed that such behavior was central to the social organization of primitive society. Malinowski's field descriptions gave anthropology an understanding of relationships between such phenomena as economics, inheritance, and the behavior between kin statuses. Radcliffe-Brown (1924) compared the sister's son–mother's brother relationship in societies with descent through females to those with descent through males. The comparison yielded generalizations comparable to ones such as Boyle's Laws in the natural sciences.

Kroeber later modified his views of kinship terminology and recognized terms as more than linguistic phenomenon. His 1909 analysis, however, has had a lasting influence on the field. Current studies of cognition that focus on a semantic analysis of kin terminology have a close relation with linguistics. A process known as componential analysis determines the meaning of terms by analyses of how relatives are grouped. The methods for classifying relatives give insight into how people view not only their relatives but also other parts of their world. Componential analysis should reveal general principles of classification which may order other aspects of a peoples' experience. Goodenough (1951, 1956b) and Lounsbury (1956) provide the methodology for expanding Kroeber's basic idea and deserve much credit for reviving it. Their work is part of a new direction in anthropology marked by Levi-Strauss (1963) who had sought to construct formal models based on probing into the unconscious mind of various peoples. He ranged over an array of materials from face paintings to mythology, but a lack of complete data often blocked a full analysis. In pursuing similar formal analyses, Americans focused on kinship terminology, an area where data were relatively abundant. A special edition of the *American Anthropologist* (Vol. 67, No. 5, Part 2) exemplifies the method. As yet, it is highly intricate and even lacks a standard notational system. However, it is an important new development and the preliminary steps in componential analysis are introduced in Part Two of this text.

By contrast, early workers saw terminology simply as an extension of inter-personal behavior. Radcliffe-Brown (1924) notes that aborigines classified many logically different types of people into one group on a principle of "equivalence of brothers." If one regards the father's brother as a father, then father's brother's sons become relatives of the same kind as one's brother. The "principle" was further analyzed by Malinowski (1927) and Evans-Pritchard (1929). Their argument was that a child develops certain feelings or sentiments toward members of the nuclear family. These feelings are then "extended" toward more remote relatives who are seen in a similar way to the child. The "extension hypothesis" rarely yields a full explanation of terminologies, but Schneider (1968) has revised the approach in order to consider psychological factors basic to the symbolism of American kinship.

Using extensively the work of these early British anthropologists, modern social anthropologists have been working out correlations between kinship systems and other forms of behavior. Gibbs (1964) notes that this work has been either "matrix-centered" or "kinship-centered." Matrix-centered work shows how economic, political, or other major institutions explain kinship behavior. A kinship-centered approach explains one aspect of kinship in terms of another; generalizations developed about the relation between practices such as descent and residence can be quite precise. Murdock (1949) worked out a large number of correlations, in the process developing a number of "theorems." These theorems are useful for illustrating the extent of predictability in the social sciences. Fox (1967) offers one of the most recent surveys of the field, and further provides a link between kinship and ethology. The study of free ranging primates indicates close social binds, much like kinship, must have existed even before the appearance of mankind.

In short, kinship analysis continually emphasizes how basic it is to the various parts of culture. In any discussion of kinship some mention must be made of religion, politics, education, and other facets of culture. One simply cannot describe fully the kinship practices of any society without reference to most other aspects of culture. It then becomes clear that different culture complexes are but part of an overall pattern. It follows that the behavior learned in kinship interaction will occur in other parts of a culture, and Hsu (1965, 1970) has initiated study of the correlation between kinship behavior and personality.

An interesting indication of the field's importance is that three books appeared in 1968 with the same title, *Kinship and Social Organization* (Bohannan and Middleton; Buchler and Selby; Rivers). Only the titles are the same. Bohannan and Middleton have gathered classic articles on recurrent problems that provide an important stocktaking of the field. Buchler and Selby also provide some background for general problems; however, their emphasis is much more upon contemporary theory and the use of mathematical solutions to kinship problems. The book further provides an introduction to componential analysis. Rivers' book is a reprint of *Kinship and Social Organization* published in 1914 plus his classic article, "The Genealogical Method of Anthropological Inquiry." Raymond Firth and David Schneider provide commentaries that add to the value of the book as a part of anthropology's history.

Without doubt kinship remains a central problem in the theory of anthropology. As W. H. R. Rivers (1910) found, the collection of kinship terms and behavior provides easy access to informants. More importantly it takes the investigator to the core of everyday behavior and gives insight into a society's principles of classification. The importance of kinship is illustrated by an anecdote about Australian aborigines. Supposedly when aborigines meet, they immediately determine how they are related. Until they know their relationship, they have absolutely no basis for exchange. When aborigines met Europeans and could trace no bond of kin, they might kill them, since a nonrelative was in a class with nonhumans. The accuracy of the story is not as important as the point that kinship is central in the lives of most peoples. The rules of behavior and the rules for classifying not only are extensive but also govern one's relationships with all other people. In fieldwork the anthropologist often hears, "We are all relatives here." It is his task to trace the relationships and understand the basis for them. Hopefully, study of this manual will help potential anthropologists prepare for that task.

PART ONE

CLASSIFICATIONS
OF KINSHIP SYSTEMS

Kinship as a System

A NOTABLE FIRST STEP in any science is to discover system in what appears to be diversity. As world explorers piled up ethnographic fact after fact, mankind appeared more and more diverse. In one place men exchanged sisters in marriage; elsewhere men selected cousins as mates. A mass of exotic customs stressed the differences among men. Anthropology saw its assignment as sorting the exotic details into systems and finding regularity at a more general level. Initially the study of religious practices, such as totemism, well illustrated that widely different practices varied only in detail but actually showed similarity at a more general level. Specific totems numbered in the hundreds, but very frequently totems related in the same general way to social groups.

However, far more regular and recurrent behavior may be observed in how a person classifies his relatives. In the study of kinship one finds complex sets of status relations that are duplicated time and again on continent after continent. Anthropologists have spent much effort in devising methods to classify these systems. The methods are still cumbersome and require patience to learn. Part One provides explanations and exercises to teach the methods of classifying. One should heed this warning of Lowie and Eggan (1965:378), "None of these formulations is an entirely satisfactory classification . . . since they are not as yet based on an adequate comparison of whole kinship systems in relationship to total social structures." But these classifications have provided a base for the most important anthropological theory. To understand theory it is essential to know these classifications of kinship systems.

Elements of Kinship

The *nuclear family,* consisting of parents and children, is the basis for kinship in nearly all societies, but the organization and behavior of members may vary considerably from what Americans or Europeans expect. For instance, the nuclear family may live in the household of the wife's mother as an integral part of a larger group; kin other than parents may care for or discipline the children; and economic support of the family is not always the responsibility of the father. Eggan (Eggan, Goody, and Pitt-Rivers 1968) provides further details. Although such diverse behavior is found, the structure of the nuclear family remains. It provides a beginning point for almost all kinship systems.

The nuclear family is formed by two different kinds of relationships. The marital tie of the parents is called an *affinal* relation. It is a legal tie created by marriage. Upon marriage, a man makes an affinal tie not only with his wife but also with her parents, brothers, and sisters. The parents are related to their children in a different way. Social scientists describe this biological link as a *consanguineal* relationship. In short, the nuclear family is composed of *affinal* (marital or legal) and *consanguine* (biological) ties of kinship. All peoples have recognized these differences partly by their kinship terms. They further recognize the contractual nature of affinal ties and realize they can be broken while consanguine relations are a matter of birth and are almost never broken. Finally, they recognize that the biological tie is based in part on the legal tie, and children whose parents are not married generally differ in status from children whose parents are married.

A large number of societies recognize a third category of relatives, *pseudo-kin*. *Fictive* relations are one type of pseudo-kin; adopted children are an example. In some societies slaves are incorporated into kinship systems by fiction. Another pseudo-relation is *ritual* kinship. A *compadrazgo* system, or godparenthood, is important in kinship systems throughout Latin America (Mintz and Wolf 1950; Altschuler 1965; Kottak 1967). In many parts of the world men become "blood" brothers by ritual creation of a tie.

Pseudo-relations have been surveyed by Pitt-Rivers (Eggan, Goody, and Pitt-Rivers 1968). His bibliography supplements the above citations. A related problem students may explore is the exceptional society that seems to lack nuclear families. Although exceptions seldom prove a rule, they generally provide greater understanding. The Nayar of India are best known for lacking nuclear families. Here, the core of family life appears to be a woman and her children. Of course, there is a rich family life, but its form is so unusual that the presence of a nuclear family as defined above is questionable. Gough (Schneider and Gough 1961) provides details and is a useful starting point for a research paper on kinship or on family life.

Diagramming Kinship Ties

Diagrams of kinship ties are much more convenient than verbal descriptions. It takes only a little practice to understand and use the diagrams. They allow one to see immediately how statuses are linked in terms of generation and consanguinity or affinity. In analysis of many different systems indication of precise status relation is necessary. For instance, it is possible to name precisely any relative with the *primary kin types* of "father," "mother," "husband," "wife," "brother," "sister," "son," and "daughter" terms. In a complex relationship such as "mother's brother's daughter" each primary kin type is a *point* in a *denotative range*. Stating the denotative range exactly is essential. For instance, in many societies one regards a mother's brother as a radically different relative from a father's brother. A person may be indebted to his mother's brother for his future possessions and position. The father's brother may be regarded as similar to older brother and be of no consequence in a person's economic or social life. Americans, of course, place both men in the same category by calling them "uncle." However, one should note that there is an important potential status difference between them. It is possible that the father's brother could become one's father or stepfather, but the mother's brother could never become one's father because he cannot marry his sister. In some societies this difference is explicitly recognized and father's brother is expected to marry the widow.

The foregoing is meant to illustrate the necessity for precision in designating relationships. Analysis of kinship soon leads to talk of relationships as complex as a mother's mother's brother's daughter's daughter. At this point one begins concentrating and mumbling, "My mother's–mother's–brother's—what?" A diagram does much to clarify the confusion.

Think of the various factors involved in the above relationship. Sex is obviously one, generation another. The difference between affinal and consanguine ties must also be distinguished. The Mars and Venus symbols of the biologist, ♂ and ♀, are inconvenient; anthropologists use a triangle for male, a circle for female. One line indicates consanguinity, two parallel lines affinity. Generation is determined by relative position with children placed below parents.

△ male   = affinal or marital tie
O female   —— consanguineal tie

EXERCISE 1   Use these symbols to diagram a nuclear family of father, mother, brother, and sister. Label the symbols "father," "mother," "brother," and "sister."

The diagram you constructed should have looked like this.

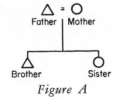

Figure A

Is this diagram the only possibility? Would the following diagram be an incorrect solution?

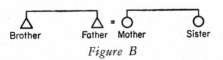

Figure B

On the basis of the information provided, Figure B is reasonable although it is not a nuclear family. In order to introduce precision, the system must be seen from the viewpoint of an individual within it. It is in the nature of kin relations that all ambiguity is removed by viewing relationships from a status within the system. This point is elementary and must be thoroughly understood. The system must be entered at one point and viewed only from that point. To indicate the point of entry one of the symbols is labeled EGO or the symbol may be shaded. In the following diagram, there can be no confusion over terms. The man labeled "father" may also be a brother, son, and uncle, but in terms of the diagram he is only a father. His status within the diagram is determined solely by his relationship with ego because it is ego's eyes that view the system.

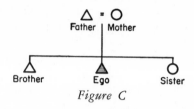

Figure C

In diagrams, ego is generally an adult unmarried male although female egos are frequently necessary also. The unmarried status allows the inclusion of most consanguine relatives without cluttering the diagram with affinals. But adult males do marry and become a member of a second nuclear family; thus, man is forced into coping with the problems that arise from membership in two nuclear families. For instance where is the new family to reside? How does one suddenly cease being only a son and become a husband and father? What will be the tie of the new family to wife's family and to husband's family? Man has found various solutions to these problems, but everywhere men have much in common because of their membership in two families.

In Figure C ego's family consists solely of his consanguine kin, his parents and *siblings* (a shorthand term for brothers and sisters). In this family, ego learns most of his culture; family members shape his personality; and he is oriented toward adult life. Anthropologists term it a *family of orientation*. When ego creates a new nuclear family by marrying, a major part of his role is the procreation and rearing of children. For ego, it is a *family of procreation*. The bearing and rearing of children, who are consanguines, is highly important, but a major feature of this family is the affinal tie to spouse and many of her relatives.

EXERCISE 2   Construct a diagram showing both ego's family of orientation and procreation. Draw a solid circle around the family of orientation, a broken circle around the family of procreation. Answers to the exercises are at the end of the book.

Abbreviations in Kinship

Kinship diagrams in print must be small to conserve space. Labeling the diagram requires abbreviations, and this usage frequently occurs in text. As a result, phrases like *"ate*=FaPaSbSo, FaMoBr, FaSiDaSo" are common in the literature (Matthews 1959).

The abbreviations are simply the first two letters of the shortened word. Fa=father, Si=sister, So=son. A few words, such as sibling=Sb, are abbreviated differently to avoid confusion. Most abbreviations are quite clear but some may be initially confusing: Pa=parents, Hu=husband, Ch=child, Sp=spouse, and La=in-law. These abbreviations are well worth the short time it takes to become familiar with them.

The abbreviations of English terms are not wholly sufficient. Anthropologists sometimes must add to the list because other peoples classify relatives in quite different ways. For instance, a man may call his MoBr by one term while his sister uses a completely different term for the same person. American speakers are slightly familiar with the practice since a woman may refer to her father as "daddy" while a man would hardly think of using the term. This problem of terminology is solved in print by the use of initials *m* or *f* preceding the kinship term. For example, mMoBr indicates the term used by a male speaker for mother's brother; fMoBr is used by a female speaker. Many peoples also indicate whether a relative in the same generation is older or younger than ego. The relative age of siblings is frequently noted, and the anthropologist may use the abbreviation Br(e), meaning term for elder brother, or Si(y) meaning younger sister. The relative age of a point in a denotative range can also be designated. Fa(e)BrWi means "father's elder brother's wife." Appropriate abbreviations for unusual circumstances are generally supplied in the particular ethnographic text, but technical articles often assume readers are familiar with a wide range of practice in abbreviating.

It must be emphasized throughout the study of kinship that precision in terminology is necessary because native kin terms are clues to behavior and cognition patterns. Terminology is generally the single best index of behavior that an anthropologist can find. Frequently, the terminology indicates social structure that is the foundation for the totality of social organization. Furthermore, kinship terminologies have been the richest source of data for semantic analysis and insight into how peoples think or give meaning to words.

Despite the importance of kinship, anthropologists have neglected to standardize abbreviations. Other systems are quite common and the student should be familiar with them. One system uses S for sister and s for son. To be consistent, capitals are used for the same and above generations; small letters are used for generations below ego. This practice results in: "bankil [is a term for] mFBs(e), mB(e), mMSs(e), mMBds(e), mMBsds(e)" (Hopkins 1969:86). The initial term, mFBs(e), stands for male speaking, father's brother's son, older than ego. In another system English anthropologists use all single capitals distinguishing sister from son by using Z for the former and S for son.

TABLE 1
SUMMARY OF ABBREVIATIONS

Primary Kin Types		Usages	
father	Fa	F	F
mother	Mo	M	M
husband	Hu	H	H
wife	Wi	W	W
brother	Br	B	B
sister	Si	Z	S
son	So	S	s
daughter	Da	D	d

EXERCISE 3 Label the following diagram with appropriate abbreviations. Do not use terms such as uncle; be specific using FaBr or MoBr. It is often essential to think in terms of a FaSiDa rather than cousin. This exercise is meant to develop such thinking. Use two of the three forms of abbreviation introduced above.

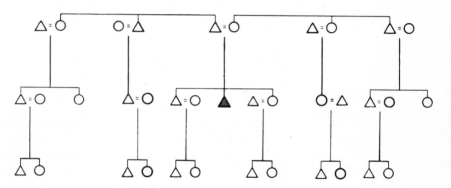

American Kinship

Exercise 3 was meant as practice for labeling relatives with precision. Although the compounded, descriptive terms are derived from English, they are not the terms ordinarily used by English speakers. In Exercise 4 use the regular English terms, such as "uncle" or "cousin," that *you* would employ in referring to relatives. For simplicity a number of possible relationships have been omitted.

EXERCISE 4 Write the English term you would use if you were ego in referring to these relatives, that is, in saying "He (She) is my _____."

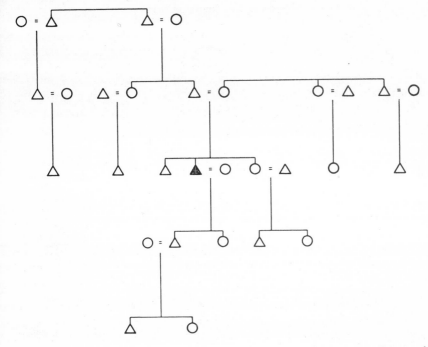

No one correct answer is supplied for this problem because English speakers, like other peoples, vary in their terminology. One person may describe a relative as a "cousin once removed" while another calls this relative a "second cousin." The reasons for this variation are not well understood. An initial study by Schneider and Homans (1955) raises as many questions as it answers. A componential analysis of American kinship (Goodenough 1965) serves as a good introduction to the methodology but yields only one model of the American system. In a critique of Goodenough, David Schneider (1965, 1968) refers to new data that provide an extensive analysis of American kin behavior as a symbol system. The familiar subject matter of these studies allows beginners to follow the exposition and much of the theory.

Other alternative kinship terms arise depending upon whether ego is talking *to* or *about* his relatives. One is likely to refer to one's "father," but he will say "Dad, can I have the car tonight?" A *term of reference* is used in referring to father; a *term of address* or *vocative* is used in speaking to father. In collecting kinship terms it is important to record both terms of address and reference. Most systems show more differences between the terms than does the American system. Most often analyses of terminology are based only on reference terms, but occasionally address terminology may follow a different system and should also be analyzed (Conant 1961).

A major difficulty encountered in the exercise is FaFaBrSo. Is he a cousin, second cousin, or a cousin once removed? What is ego's FaFaBrSoSo? Is he not the second cousin? There can be no standard answer for these questions because Americans simply do not agree on terminology. Cousins at this distance tend to "fade out" (Schneider 1965) or jokingly become "kissing cousins." However, in some other societies people regard a FaFaBrSoSo as a close, important relative and may refer to him by the same term they use for brother.

Further study of the diagram reveals other details characteristic of kinship systems. Examine the full meanings of each of the terms. For instance, what does "aunt" denote? It specifies both sex and generation. An aunt is a female relative in my parent's generation; an anthropologist might designate aunt as a female in the first ascending generation. The term further indicates a relative who is a sibling of a parent or the spouse of a parental sibling. Almost all American terms denote not only the sex of a relative but also generation relative to ego (that is, same, first ascending, or first descending). Any number of generations beyond these can be specified by use of "grand" or "great." Since peoples all over the world have divided work and activities along generation and sex lines, it is not surprising that kinship terms denote these criteria also. As indicated above there are other criteria such as relative age, sex of speaker, or even whether a relative is living or dead. Of course all the principles need not be operative for all terms. Some American kinship terms do not denote sex.

Although most people recognize immediately that cousin seems unique as including both males and females, there are terms such as spouse, child, parent, and sibling that also fail to denote sex. It may seem "uncomfortable" to include these latter terms with cousin. Goodenough (1965) notes that these terms differ from the ones you probably wrote into Exercise 4. Since they are at a higher level of abstraction, they are often excluded from lists of terms such as "husband," "son" or "mother."

The exercise illustrates another aspect of kinship important to anthropology. Note that direct ascendants and descendants—Fa, FaFa, FaMo, Mo, MoFa, MoMo, So, Da, SoSo, and SoDa—are all differentiated in terminology from relatives to the side, such as uncles or nieces. Persons in the direct consanguineal lines are known technically as *lineal* relatives; the relatives to the sides are called *collateral* relatives. English terms sharply separate collaterals from lineals. In the first ascending generation all collaterals are lumped as uncle and aunt or a type of cousin (for example, FaFaBrSo); in ego's generation all collaterals are cousins; in the first descending generation they are nephews and nieces or a type of cousin. Ego's siblings may be considered either lineals or collaterals; their anomalous position need not be resolved here. It is important to realize that American terminology reinforces behavior and belief that lineals are somehow "naturally" different from collaterals. Many kinship systems fail to distinguish between lineal and collateral relatives and initially they may be confusing. It must be emphasized, *there is nothing natural about separating lineal from collateral relatives* either in terminology or behavior. It is simply that Americans and Europeans are accustomed to only this system and assume it is part of human nature.

Finally, the exercise is intended to illustrate one of the most important aspects of kinship study. Terminology reveals much about human thought. The emphasis on lineal relatives indicates the symbolic importance of the nuclear family to Americans, for instance. Schneider and Homans' analysis (1955:1199) also suggests subtle behavior patterns, such as female subordination. Study of termi-

nology can seldom prove such a feature as sex subordination, but it does give clues
to patterns of behavior and modes of classification.

EXERCISE 5   Anthropologists frequently use lineal and collateral as technical terms in describing kinship systems. Distinguish the lineal relatives in the
following diagram by darkening the appropriate symbols.

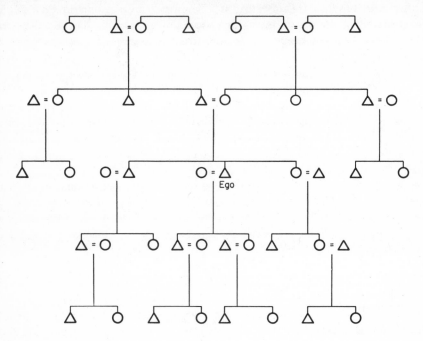

Other Kinship Systems

Students must be aware that their own kinship system is so taken for
granted that other systems will at first seem bizarre, irrational, and difficult to
appreciate. Everywhere children begin learning their kinship system at birth. Many
of their first words are kinship terms; the people who care for them are all relatives. The kin words become essential guides to action because they place persons
in categories and assign statuses. As Fortes (1969:54) phrases it, a kinship word
"is a package of definitions, rules and directions for conduct. It is a store of information but also a tool of action." Logically it would seem that each society might
develop its own particular system or "package of definitions," but the remarkable
fact about kinship is that of all the logical possibilities man employs only a few.

A simple one to understand occurs in much of Oceania and in a number of
other places around the world. It is a system that does not distinguish between
lineal and collateral relatives. One term is used for all the males in ego's generation,
another term for all the females. One term suffices for all the women in the first
ascending generation, another for the men. This system poses a problem in trans-

lating for English speakers. How will a term for the males in ego's generation be translated? Missionaries who wrote most early dictionaries needed a term for the English "brother." With some logic, they equated the term "male in ego's generation," but this choice meant that cousins, also males in ego's generation, were the same as brothers. A translation of the foreign term into nearest English categories distorts the meaning. It is difficult initially to think of a system where all the male "cousins" are "brothers" because that is a semantic contradiction in English. An even greater difficulty occurs in the first ascending generation. The English term "father" denotes one and only one person. In a dictionary the term for "male in first ascending generation" again is translated logically as "father." When the same term also is the translation for uncle (there is simply no other kinship term available in English), it becomes necessary to describe the system as showing all the uncles as "father," again misleading. An alternative is to use the original native terms in order to avoid the misleading denotations of the English terms. The introduction of foreign languages, however, raises numerous problems and disadvantages. The compromise employed here is to use letter symbols. What is important to realize is that the same symbol for different relatives simply indicates they are called by the same term. English terminology would appear as the following symbol system.

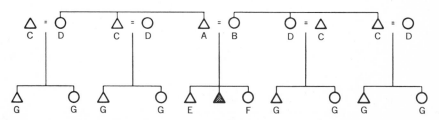

Figure D. English terminology converted to symbols.

The system from Oceania, described before, simply designates sex and generation; it is sometimes called *generational*. Note how it classifies relatives quite differently from the system pictured above.

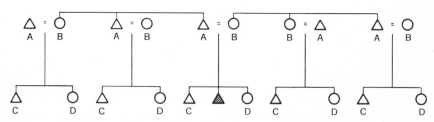

Figure E. Generational terminology converted to symbols.

In a system like that diagrammed above, the word for "B" is generally translated as "mother." One of the first questions is: Do they really think they have more than one mother? It must be understood that "mother" is simply a near English equivalent term or gloss in translating; the original native term does not have the same connotations as the English word. In such a system the women who stand as a "kind of mother" to ego all behave toward him in much the same way. The system maximizes the social role of motherhood while minimizing the biological role.

"Father," likewise, has been glossed to include the brothers of a father. That is, the Melanesian word *tama* is generally translated as "father" because Melanesians were first asked, "What is your term for father?" Then when asked, "What is your term for father's brother?" and they replied "*tama*," anthropologists explained that the term for father was extended to father's brother. Even though Hocart (1937) long ago noted such glossing was quite misleading, many anthropologists continued the practice. Only recently would *tama* regularly be translated as something like "males of the first ascending generation on the father's side."

American and Other Marriage Systems

American marriage practices may be described as complex because of extensive variation or because of diverse psychological factors, but most Western marriages are remarkably simple sociologically because they often affect only the spouses. Almost nowhere, except in parts of the urban industrialized world, is marriage simply a union between spouses; it is also, and primarily, an alliance or union between groups. If one assumes marriage is for alliance purposes, one can appreciate how a marriage could be arranged between a bride and groom who have never met, as happens in much of the world. The two are delegates from their groups who form a pact like a political union. The marriage does not require love and companionship; these qualities can be found in the original groups and the two will continue their memberships there.

Marriage as alliance also explains the wide spread distribution of the *sororate* and *levirate*. The sororate is a norm that directs a man to marry the sister of his deceased wife. It is not usually necessary to marry an actual sister but someone "like a sister," someone who is a member of the wife's group, someone who will keep the alliance intact. Similarly, the levirate is a practice that provides a widow with a "brother" of her deceased husband, but the expected marriage of the widow within the group is more than a remarriage just for her sake. The levirate serves as insurance that an alliance created by one marriage will not be dissolved by the death of one person. Westerners may be familiar with the customs of levirate and sororate through the Old Testament.

Since one custom is just the converse of the other, the practices may be confused if one is not careful. Study Figure F to remember the differences. An X denotes a death.

Westerners generally puzzle over the practices because they ask, "What if a person doesn't have any unmarried siblings?" Recall how a generational system provides many "siblings" because cousins become brothers and sisters. In the levirate a widow may marry anyone who was like a brother to her deceased husband. Further, the levirate and sororate are usually forms of *preferential* marriage. It is a desired or ideal form, but other unions are allowed. Or a "brother" or "sister" of

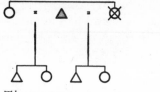 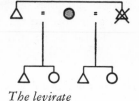

Figure F.   *The sororate*   *The levirate*

the deceased spouse may be created through fictive means in order to continue the alliance properly. Occasionally, the customs may be *prescribed* with no alternatives available; if no proper spouse is available then remarriage is impossible.

Expectation or *requirement* are the important qualities that constitute norms such as the levirate or sororate. Occasionally a Western woman marries her dead husband's brother. Such a case is not the levirate because only personal choice directed such a marriage. If the practice were to become regular because people thought or said it was a "good thing" or it "ought to be that way," the practice would be *institutionalized*. The levirate would become normative.

Kinship Classifications

The above marriage practices will be used shortly to explain some kinship classifications. One should note first that anthropologists see so much regular, recurrent behavior in kinship that they describe it as a system. Further they find similar systems throughout the world. A primary task, therefore, is to devise an appropriate classification of the various kinship systems. As yet the classifications are not as useful as the ones biologists devised in the nineteenth century. However, much work has been accomplished in constructing two taxonomic schemes. Students of social anthropology must be familiar with both of them.

As an introduction it is useful to start with Morgan's (1870) attempt at a taxonomy. He divided all the systems simply into two general groups, *descriptive* and *classificatory*. A descriptive system was one that distinguished lineal from collateral relatives. Western systems of terminology are descriptive. Classificatory systems grouped or lumped collateral relatives with lineal ones. The generational system described above equated collaterals with lineals. Morgan further saw differences among classificatory systems; in some of the systems only half of the collaterals were equated with lineals. Morgan's final classification reflects his ethnocentrism, but his first attempt to classify kinship systems became a classic.

A major refinement in taxonomy has been provided by Robert Lowie and Paul Kirchoff who examined ego's terminology for parental siblings. They were particularly interested in the systems lying between Morgan's classificatory and descriptive extremes. In many societies ego's FaBr and Fa are referred to by the same term, but MoBr has a different term. In a few societies each of these men has a separate term of reference. In the former case the system is termed *bifurcate merging*; in the latter case it is *bifurcate collateral*. A Western system is still described as lineal; Morgan's term "classificatory" is replaced by *generational*. The taxonomy is actually quite simple when shown through diagrams.

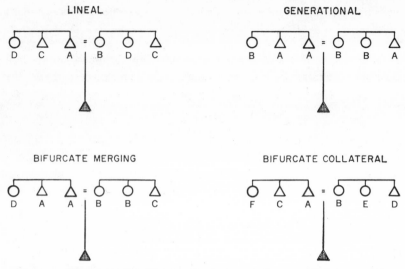

Figure G. Classification by first ascending generation.

A further refinement of taxonomy concentrated on analysis of the terms for cousins and siblings. Leslie Spier (1925) and George Murdock (1949) have used this taxonomy extensively. A lineal system, the one familiar to Westerners but comparatively rare in the rest of the world, separates all cousins from siblings. On the basis of cousin terminology it is known as an *Eskimo* system. A generation system that equates all cousins with siblings is called an *Hawaiian* system. The words *Eskimo* and *Hawaiian* apply to systems of terminology, not just to two particular societies. That is, American society is said to have an Eskimo system of kinship terminology while a few Eskimo groups actually do not have an Eskimo system.

A system of bifurcate collateral terminology for the first ascending generation usually means that each cousin will be distinguished from the other as well as from siblings. Where there are separate terms for FaSiCh, FaBrCh, Br, MoSiCh, and MoBrCh, the system is called *Sudanese*. This system is comparatively rare.

The parallels between lineal and Eskimo, generational and Hawaiian, bifurcate collateral and Sudanese are clear. The advantage of a classification based on cousins lies in further refinement of bifurcate merging systems. The cousin system provides for three different systems under the bifurcate merging category. These three are *Iroquois*, *Crow* and *Omaha*. To understand these systems it is necessary to introduce some distinctions among cousins that most peoples of the world always make, but initially the differences confuse Western students.

Cousin Relations

Bifurcate merging systems where FaBr is equated with father and MoSi with mother are prevalent around the world. This pair of relations is so frequently grouped with ego's parents that they deserve special designation. Anthropologists call them the parallel aunt and uncle. That is, FaBr and MoSi are the parallel uncle and aunt.

If these relatives are in a category with ego's own parents, it is logical that their children will be in the same category as ego's siblings. In a sense the children of parallel uncles and aunts are ego's brothers and sisters whenever FaBr=Fa and MoSi=Mo. Anthropologists describe these kin with the technical term *parallel cousins*.

EXERCISE 6   Draw a diagram showing parallel cousins. Label the appropriate relatives Mo, Fa, Br, Si, but remember these terms can only be rough translations of native terms. The glosses will be misleading if you think of them simply as extensions.

The answer for this exercise at the back omits labels for FaBrWi and for MoSiHu. Since the wife of FaBr is a woman married to ego's "father," she may be called "mother." However, affinal terminology is not so consistent as consanguine terminology, and the term for FaBrWi may be a highly descriptive term that can only be translated as "father's wife."

The relatives MoBr and FaSi are the ones that are separated in special categories in many societies. Technically, they are described as the *cross uncle* and *cross aunt*; their children become *cross cousins* to ego. Ego's MoSiCh and FaBrCh are *parallel cousins*. In other words, children of siblings of the same sex are parallel cousins to each other; children of siblings of opposite sex are cross cousins to each other.

EXERCISE 7   Draw a diagram showing ego's parallel cousins and cross cousins. Indicate cross cousins by an X; parallel cousins by //. These are symbols generally used by anthropologists to indicate the cross and parallel type of relation.

No one is certain why these distinctions are made by so many peoples, but a particular case may give some understanding. Among Dakota Indians two brothers share many activities such as work, travel, or attending a meeting. Their children often accompany them and are therefore in close contact like brothers. Similarly sisters often participate together in activities bringing their children together. Thus the children of siblings of the same sex are often together like brothers and sisters. Very seldom do adult brother and sister engage in the same event; thus children of siblings of opposite sex are not often brought together.

Although this explanation is only partial, it should give some appreciation for equating parallel cousins with siblings while the cross-cousins fall in a different category. Such a system, the most common in terms of numbers of societies, is known as an *Iroquois* system. To demarcate clearly cross cousins, as so many systems do, it is convenient to draw diagrams so that the cross cousins are located to the extreme left and right of ego.

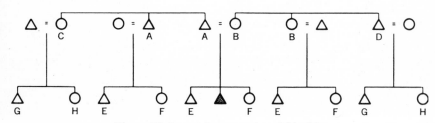

Figure H. Iroquois categories of kinship.

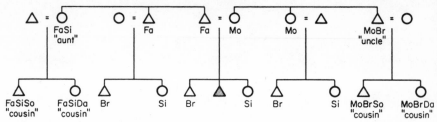

Figure I. Iroquois terminology translated into nearest English equivalents.

Classification of kinship systems by *cousin terminology* is relatively simple for the four types described above. *In the Eskimo system all cousins are equated with each other but differentiated from siblings.* Such a system generally coincides with lineal terminology for first ascending generation. *In a Hawaiian system all cousins are equated with siblings.* In effect, there are no cousin terms. *In a Sudanese system there are separate terms for each of the cousins and separate terms for siblings.* The following diagrams illustrate the differences:

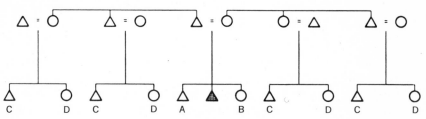

Figure J. Eskimo terminology.

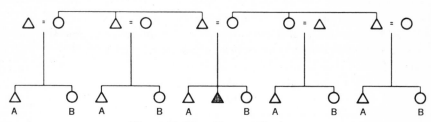

Figure K. Hawaiian terminology.

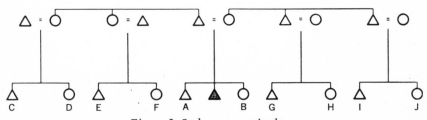

Figure L. Sudanese terminology.

Note a kind of balance in these systems because terms on the mother's side are essentially the same as those on the father's side. The terminology suggests that kinship is based on *bilateral descent*, a belief that relationships descend and ascend more or less equally through both *males and females*. It is accurate, but misleading, to describe the situation as descent from both the *father and mother*. It is misleading because kinship roles, "father" and "mother," are not part of descent beliefs; rather, the descent is linkage through the sex roles, male and female.

American kinship exemplifies ties through bilateral descent. Any woman may qualify for membership in the Daughters of the American Revolution if she has any ancestor who participated in the colonial revolt. The ascent may be traced through a mother's mother's father's mother's father, for instance. Note that the ascent shifts readily between male and female links in constructing a line of descent. It could also be through all females or all males but generally involves both sexes. Americans feel quite content in such reckoning; they even tend to believe that they are related *equally* to all their ancestors. Genetically, of course, it is nearly impossible that a person be related equally to his sixteen great-great-grandparents. After a few more generations it becomes probable that a person will not have inherited any genes from one of his ancestors. However, DAR members do not allow scientific knowledge to interfere with beliefs about descent. Indeed most people do not see genetic descent as relevant to social descent.

Under modern conditions the importance of the nuclear family makes it difficult for students to appreciate the importance of descent lines and the wide network of kin provided by ancestors for most other peoples. Bohannan (1963:127) describes how Anglo-Saxons in medieval times were obligated to sixth cousins. Imagine the number of ancestors and descendants involved. At some point, however, relationships had to be severed. All kinship systems must solve the problem of excluding some relatives while including others. Anglo-Saxon limits were placed by limiting the number of generations used for reckoning relationships. Most other peoples have set limits by including only relatives who have a common ancestor *and* can trace ascent to him only through one sex. Such a system is so different in belief and consequence from the Western one that initially it can be most confusing. In large part the confusion lies in the student's assumption that the other system is somehow "unnatural." However, anthropologists most often find that peoples trace descent and ascent through only one sex. When the tracing is through males, or *ancestors*, the practice is said to be *patrilineal* or "through the father," but it is more accurate to think of it as through *males*. Thus, the word *agnatic* is preferable. In the literature one will see both *patrilineal* and *agnatic*. When ascent is through females or *ancestresses*, the practice is called *matrilineal; uterine* is the preferred alternative. In either agnatic or uterine descent a group of kin is singled out that anthropologists term a unilineal descent group. Such descent does not exclude persons on the other side as *unrelated*; these relatives are simply of a different nature because they are excluded from the descent group.

In systems such as these, ideas of descent are distinct from those of Europeans. Where descent is uterine the male's role in procreation is thought to be minimal. A man may simply "open" a woman to allow conception by spiritual means. Obviously doctrines of procreation are important for understanding descent beliefs. Bohannan (1963:133–136) describes a number of other beliefs about conception and their relation to various descent rules.

Unilineal Descent

Many factors play a part in unilineal descent. The most obvious are certain residence patterns which correlate highly with certain forms of descent. In turn, both descent and residence are tied in complex ways to ecology and the control of economic goods. Turner (1969:82–84) provides an example where ecology distributes the Ndembu over a wide area with couples living alternately with the husband's and wife's groups. Unlike many neighboring, more stable groups, Ndembu descent is irregular. Sahlins (1961) examines the function of descent groups in expanding into other territories. Unilineal systems in general are surveyed by Freedman (1965) and Goody (Eggan, Goody, and Pitt-Rivers 1968). It seems likely that anthropology will have to devise further classifications of descent groups before their relationship with economics and residence patterns are understood fully.

An initial understanding of unilineal systems can begin with the Washo Indians. Downs (1966) divides the aboriginal Washo year into fishing, hunting, and gathering times. Men did almost all the hunting. Fishing was also a male activity, but a wife helped in preparing for fishing. Women did most of the gathering, but husbands often joined their wives at the end of the fishing season. Generally a Washo man taught hunting techniques and the boy acquired detailed knowledge of his father's hunting territory. The mother taught her daughter gathering techniques, and the women acquired customary rights over berry patches or pinon trees. Each sex contributed about half of the subsistence. What happens when the children marry? Will the son inherit rights to his father's hunting territory and remain there, bringing in a wife to replace his sister as gatherer? Or will the son leave and allow his sister's husband to acquire the hunting territory? No regular rules were institutionalized by the Washo and neither inheritance nor descent became fixed in one sex. The important kin for the Washo were the immediate bilateral relatives.

Contrast these people with the horticultural Huron Indians described by Trigger (1969). Women spend most of their time in the field, helped by men with the heavy work. Subsistence is mainly from the fields but men add meat and fish. Their activities take them over a wide area. The local vested interest is in the fields where daughters accompany their mothers. A woman could pass on this interest to her son's wife, but a daughter already knows the field. More importantly she knows how to get along with mother. Consistently daughters are likely to remain at home; males will settle in their wives' households. The Longhouse or household consists of a woman, her daughters and their husbands, and their daughters and unmarried sons. Only the husbands of these women are in the household through affinal ties, and they usually have no relationship to each other.

One should analyze this situation thoroughly to appreciate the positions of men and women. An adult male marries and moves into a household occupied by his wife, her mother, her sisters, and her unmarried brothers. Most other adult males in the household are in the same position as he is—a virtual stranger. If trouble occurs with the wife, the man has a host of consanguine relatives allied against him. For solace he must remain tied to his mother's household and his own lineage; the situation reemphasizes the importance of the female line. Ego's position may be understood better by completing Exercise 8. Many of the implications for these relationships were set forth initially by Malinowski (1927, 1929). Barnett (1960) and Dozier (1966) provide further descriptions, especially written for students.

EXERCISE 8   Ego marries into a household organized around uterine relatives. Shade all the consanguine relatives of ego's wife. Note that all of these relatives are linked through females.

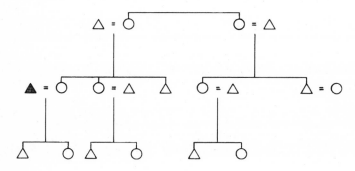

Note that almost all of these relatives will share the household with ego, that is, ego's wife's household. Which one relative will have moved out? Generally a number of factors determine actual residence. The norms, in this instance, would call for ego's WiMoSiSo to be the only relative to leave the household. He would relocate with the line of women his wife represents.

The Lineage

The group described above as a unilineal descent group is also called a *lineage*. The Huron have *matrilineages*. In short a line of females and their brothers form a group with enduring relations. The converse, a line of males and their sisters, form *patrilineages*. Pastoral peoples and intensive agriculturalists are generally patrilineal. Lineages generally control property or right to land; thus goods are usually *inherited* according to lineage membership. Lineages may also control ritual and political offices or other prestigous positions. *Succession* to these offices will be through the lineages. Therefore, control of property and membership in important political and ritual offices are largely determined by one's lineage.

The salient feature of the lineage is that many political, religious, and economic rights and goods belong to the group, not to individual members. The group assumes responsibility for the individual so that in blood feuds, for instance, the death of any group member satisfies the revenge. Americans and Europeans generally do not associate such behavior with kinship but rather with private or public corporations. Later the parallel between the lineages and corporations will be more closely drawn. Here it may be noted that lineages occur in societies with types of wealth that tend to be distributed through only one of the sexes.

Lineages unite many people over generations and frequently incorporate dead ancestors. The incorporation and veneration of the elderly and the dead ancestors may lead to a misleading conclusion that ancestors are worshipped as gods. Many cases of "ancestor worship" are probably better understood as a part of kinship rather than religious behavior.

Generally the greater the number of generations traced, the larger the number of people united within a lineage. On the other hand, lineages act as dividing forces within a society. Allegiance and responsibility to the lineage may conflict with duties toward spouse and affines or age mates. Some lineages become so powerful that they may even threaten tribal ties. Competition between lineages can also disrupt tribal cohesion.

Although lineage bonds generally are strong, a potential for splintering is inherent in lineage organization. Two or more sisters in a matrilineage are the potential for new lines. Analyze what might happen to a matrilineage when a woman has several daughters, as in Figure M.

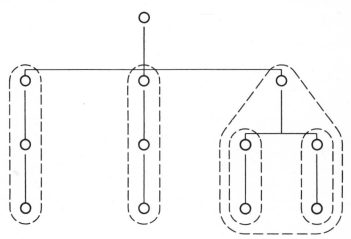

Figure M. Illustrations of inherent splintering or fission in lineage organization.

In Figure M three lines begin in the second generation and a fourth line has arisen in the third. If the oldest female ancestor shown were forgotten, then there would be at least three lineages.

It is tempting to think that many peoples have kept lineage organization intact by substituting mythical ancestors for forgotten ancestors. This substitution seems to have occurred, but anthropologists have little evidence for the actual process. That is, many peoples do relate their oldest known ancestor (the lineage founder) to a mythical being who is ancestoral to other lineage founders. This grouping is known as a *sib* or *clan*. Unfortunately, anthropologists have not standardized their usage of these two words; the glossary provides background for the usage of sib and clan. In this text clan will be used to indicate a union of two or more lineages linked to a mythical ancestor. Such union may also be provided by a real person where the descent ties are presumed but cannot be traced.

Remember that clan membership is like lineage membership; it is traced through one sex. A system through males is *agnatic* or *patrilineal*. A system that traces through females is *uterine* or *matrilineal*.

EXERCISE 9   Ego is in a matrilineage. Place a dot in all the relatives that will be in his lineage. Remember that membership in the lineage passes on through females but ends with males. That is, males will be in the matrilineage, but not their children.

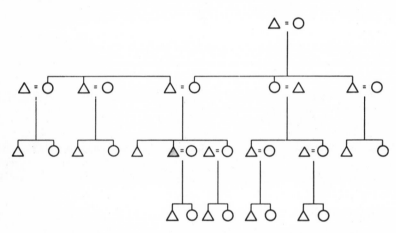

Note well that in matrilineal descent the children of a male ego are *not* in his matrilineage or clan. The children of ego's sister are in the *same* matrilineage and clan as ego. Whatever property, obligations, offices, and privileges ego has *as a clan or lineage member* cannot be passed on to his sons and daughters. Instead, a male's logical heir is his sister's son. In turn, ego cannot inherit or succeed his father but rather looks to his mother's brother. Reconsider the Huron. Here matrilineages had developed; further combinations of the lineages formed clans. In both lineage and clan, descent is through females. However, men usually control political, religious, and economic life; ritual or political offices within clans are almost always held by males. The knowledge, power, and position that must be passed on to a younger generation must also be kept within the lineage or clan. A man's own son is outside his lineage and clan; it is a man's sister's son who is the logical heir because he is within the lineage. In all matrilineal societies the mother's brother—sister's son relationship is highly important; in a number of ways the MoBr resembles Fa in a bilateral or patrilineal society. What is of particular interest is a comparison of the relationship in patrilineal societies as opposed to matrilineal ones. Radcliffe-Brown (1924) was among the first to make such comparison and analysis; Goody (1959) and Levi-Strauss (1963: 40–51) have more recently reevaluated the comparison.

In general the principles of patrilineal organization or *patriliny* are like those of *matriliny* although some major differences between the two do occur

(Schneider and Gough 1961). The two are sufficiently similar that the introduction here to patriliny will also serve as a review of matriliny. In the following exercise note that tracing descent through males gives a diagram similar, but reversed, to that of Exercise 9.

EXERCISE 10   Ego is in a patrilineage. Place a dot in all the relatives that will be in ego's lineage. They, and many others, will also be in his clan.

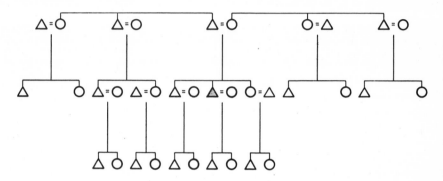

Note carefully that both sexes are included as lineage members in either matriliny or patriliny, but in a patrilineal system descent passes only through males. Female descendents will belong to the group but not their offspring. In a matrilineal system descent passes only through females. The children of males will not belong to the same descent group as their fathers.

Characteristics of the Lineage and Clan

All kin ties within a lineage or clan are consanguine. The relationship is considered a close one, and in some contexts the tie within the lineage resembles the sibling tie. Therefore, one does not marry a lineage or clan mate because relatives are considered too close. Thus, a major characteristic of lineages and clans is that they are *exogamous*. A member must marry *outside* his group. (*Endogamy* is marriage within a group. In a few exceptional societies lineages may be endogamous.) The exogamic rules for lineage and clan mean that in-laws, as well as spouse, are automatically of a group different from ego.

Another characteristic of the clan is for the mythical ancestor of the patrilineages or ancestress of the matrilineages to be a nonhuman figure. An animal is the usual founder, but plants and phenomena such as rain or thunder may also symbolize the origin of a clan. Whatever the symbol, it is known as a *totem*, from the Ojibway Indian language. Occasionally a clan is found without totems, or a real person with unusual qualities is presumed to have been a common ancestor. The widespread distribution of totems was of particular interest to early anthropologists (Levi-Strauss 1962); still there is no satisfactory explanation for the popularity of totems. Totem-like symbols may also represent other groups (Linton 1924).

Lineages and clans also have some of the characteristics of *corporate* groups. The characteristic of corporate *perpetuity* is especially useful for understanding lineage and clan organization. Just as the General Electric Corporation will "outlive" all its stockholders and officers, clans and lineages continue after the death of the individuals composing a group at any point in time. The perpetuity of clan and lineage allows major economic, political, and religious functions to be invested in them. In addition to perpetuity, lineages and clans, like other corporate groups, possess names, symbols (such as a totem pole or the GE trademark), rules of membership, and other special norms. Unlike the modern impersonal corporation, the relations with the lineage and clan are marked by affect and emotion. Over all, the clan is usually the focal point of a person's life where descent is unilineal. Clans may determine an individual's spouse, occupation, religious role, and position in the prestige system.

Kinship Systems in Unilineal Societies

If lineages are such an integral part of life, one can expect that their effects will be seen in kinship terminological systems. And, *Crow* and *Omaha* kinship systems do show a high correlation with unilineal descent. However, it should be noted immediately that unilineal descent does occur with other kinship systems, particularly Iroquois. It must also be noted that Crow or Omaha terminology may occur without unilineal descent, although unilineal descent practices in the past are suspected for any society with Crow or Omaha terms.

To understand the nature of Crow and Omaha terminology, it is useful to keep in mind characteristics of lineages and clans: (1) In some contexts, lineage and clan members *are thought of* as siblings. (2) Ego will belong to the same lineage or clan throughout life, the membership usually *determined by birth* but on rare instances achieved. (3) Still, ego is bound through a parent to another lineage and clan. That is, ego will feel a special tie to his father's lineage if in a matrilineage or to his mother's lineage if in a patrilineage. Much of the content of this relationship to the "other lineage" is in the nature of affect, emotion, and morality. The complexity of the relationship makes it variable among societies. The tie is called complementary filiation, and its nature has been discussed at length by Fortes (1959) and Schneider (1963). Although complementary filiation varies among societies, it is useful to see its effects in at least one group. Eggan (1950:111–116) provides such a description for behavior among the matrilineal Hopi. The following exercises concentrate only on showing the structure and terminology of Crow and Omaha systems.

EXERCISE 11   Ego is in a matrilineage. Place a dot in the relatives within ego's lineage. Place an X in the relatives tied to ego through complementary filiation, that is, relatives in ego's father's lineage. Keeping the characteristics of lineages in mind, now analyze what terms or what categories of kin ego may construct. Assume the basic Iroquois pattern of equating parallel cousin with siblings and FaBr=Fa, MoSi=Mo. It is the cross uncle, cross aunt, and cross cousins who

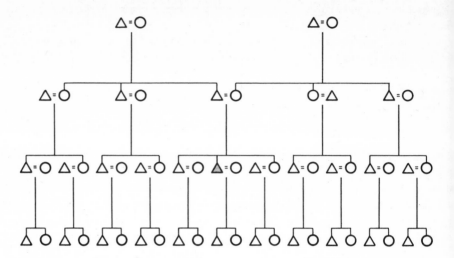

can be expected to be so different. One "uncle" will belong to ego's clan; the other cannot (note Exercise 11).

As ego matures in his mother's lineage, he must learn the male role of his lineage from his MoBr, *not* from Fa. In turn he will serve as teacher of his SiSo, *not his own So.* As the teacher or student, age differences between lineage members are important and must be maintained; the distinction between generations will be indicated in the terminology.

However, the tie of complementary filiation allows a close, warm relationship, often with fewer contacts. Relations will not be patterned subordination or superordination. In thinking of the relatives in "father's" lineage, ego may regard all of them as lineage mates of father; that is, lineage mates are like a "brother" and "sister" to father. The implied logic is that any lineage mate of father is a brother of my father, and recall that terminologically FaBr=Fa. That is, a large group of men are in the same status relation to ego, something like men of the lineage that "fathered" ego. Missionaries and others who translated native terms into English had to equate the indigenous word with the English "father." Although it is probably the closest translation, it is misleading. It is much like a Martian anthropologist who asks you what you call a MoBrSo. If he finds that you call him "cousin" and then finds that you also call MoSiSo "cousin", the Martian may report that the term for MoBrSo is extended to MoSiSo. Now, the misleading question arises: Why do you come to regard the MoSiSo as you first regarded the MoBrSo? The point is that ego is tied by complementary filiation to a group of men, *of different generations,* in the same way. He uses one term for all of them. Figure N illustrates the grouping; term "A" may be glossed as "father" but remember the gloss is only an approximation.

The terminology is so different from the usual bilateral forms that initially it is bewildering. Accounts of early European explorers who encountered such terminology are often amusing. A French explorer among the Illinois Indians described the savages as so stupid they could not remember their kinship terms; they called even small babies their "mother" who "could not possibly be their

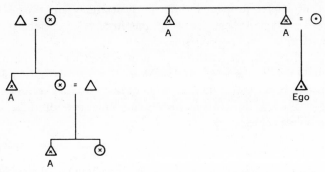

Figure N. The A category indicates that the same term will be used for all these individuals. Note that they are in different generations but all the same lineage.

mother." On the other hand, some explorers were remarkably perceptive, and Lafitau could be regarded as founding social anthropology (Tax 1955*b*) because he clearly showed many of the implications of unilineal descent. It is only necessary to accept the general principles of unilineal descent to see the logic of the terminology.

The principle of equating lineage brothers with fathers applies also to the women of father's lineage. Of course, the sex difference is noted although a native term for father's sister may sometimes be glossed as "female father." At any rate, ego sees all lineage "sisters" as the same kind of relative as FaSi, and there is only one term for all the women in this line.

EXERCISE 12   Draw a broken line around the females who are lineage sisters of ego's father. They will all be referred to by the same kinship term, "B"; label them B. Label the lineage brothers of ego's father, A, as in Figure N.

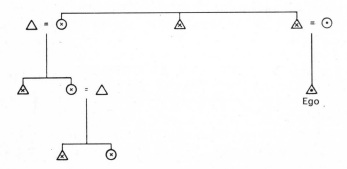

Make sure the completed answer agrees with the supplied answer at the back. Then note that a line of women, encircled by the broken line, can be quickly identified. Remember it is matrilineal terminology, but the line of women appears on ego's *father's* side.

This grouping of relatives along a line may be described as a *lineage principle*. It is in addition to principles or criteria of *sex* and *generation*. In the system described above, it may be said that the lineage principle overrides the generation principle; people of different generations are equated because they belong to the same lineage. In short, the lineage or membership criterion is more important than the criterion of generation.

Once the terms for patrilateral cousins (FaSiCh) are known, it is possible to determine logically the terms for the MoSiCh or matrilateral cross cousins. This step is possible because of a number of rules that govern kinship terminology. Sol Tax (1955a:19–23) lists twelve such rules; only two of these are needed to solve the problem above.

> a. Rule of uniform descent: If someone whom ego refers to as A has children who ego refers to as B, then the children of everybody who ego refers to as A are classified as B.
> b. Rule of uniform reciprocals: If A and B are terms used between a pair of relatives, then the reciprocal of every A must be B.

The generalization is a complex way of stating what everyone already knows implicitly. Uniform descent, for instance, is illustrated in English by aunt and cousin terminology. If somebody whom ego refers to as aunt (MoSi) has children whom ego refers to as cousin, then the children of everyone whom ego refers to as aunt (FaSi) are called cousin. The rule of uniform reciprocals is illustrated by aunt and nephew terms. Anyone ego refers to as aunt will refer to him as nephew; that is, if aunt and nephew are terms used between a pair of relatives, then the reciprocal of every aunt must be nephew. Of course, sex must also be taken into account so that niece is another reciprocal of aunt just as uncle is a reciprocal of nephew.

With these rules in mind consider the matrilateral cross cousin. The problem is: What term will ego use for MoBrSo? The solution lies in the reciprocal relation between ego and *his* FaSiSo. Ego places FaSiSo in the same category as "father"; therefore, that man will place him in the "son" category. That is, anyone I call father will call me son. Now think of ego's MoBrSo. What will that person call ego? If he puts ego in the "father" category for the same reasons ego puts his FaSiSo in that category, then what will ego call him? Ego must, of course, call

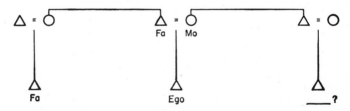

that person (the MoBrSo) "son" if that person is calling ego "father." The glosses "father" and "son" are again misleading, but they are useful for getting at the use of reciprocals in checking terminologies. Think again of ego's relation to FaSiSo. Ego groups him with father because they are both lineage mates tied to ego by filiation. Again recall the rule of uniform reciprocals; anyone I call A (loosely translated as father) will call me B (loosely translated as son). Therefore, ego's

FaSiSo calls ego "son." What is this relationship? It is a MoBrSo relation; for such a system the norm is: MoBrSo=So. Further think of the missing term in relation to ego. Ego is someone in the lineage of FaSi; therefore, he is a lineage mate of father and therefore, in a category with father. Anyone he classes with father will refer to him as son.

To test further your use of the rule of uniform reciprocity and uniform descent, supply the missing terms for the children of ego's siblings in the exercise below. Again place yourself in the numbered blanks. How will you refer to ego as you fit yourself to each blank? Ego will then refer to you by the *reciprocal*. That is, if you call him MoBr, he must call you SiSo. What he calls you is the missing term.

EXERCISE 13   Supply the terms for the blank, numbered spaces. Answers follow below.

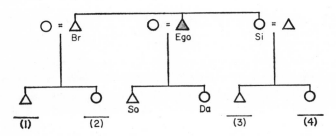

For both 1 and 2 ego is a FaBr and FaBr=Fa; therefore, he calls 1, son, and 2, daughter. Both 3 and 4 see ego as a MoBr; the reciprocals are SiSo and SiDa. The pair might also be labeled nephew and niece. Remember, however, that the English terms are only approximations to the other culture's categories. To appreciate the problem, think how misleading it would be to translate the English term "cousin" into a language where cross cousins are Fa and FaSi, So and Da, and parallel cousins equate with Br and Si.

The Crow Kinship System

The system of terminology introduced above for a matrilineage is known technically as a Crow type. Crow terminology is almost always associated with matriliny, but matrilineal societies may have Iroquois or other types, rather than Crow. However, the anthropologist does expect Crow terminology with long established matrilineages. The basic categories for Crow have been established in the above exercises. The structure so far presented is reviewed in Figure O. Note the line of women grouped together with FaSi. Also note in the diagram a number of equations that are unusual to English speakers. In English, for instance, we equate MoBrSo with FaSiSo; that is, both are "cousins." In a Crow system one term will be used for the following: Fa=FaBr=FaSiSo=FaSiDaSo; FaSi=

FaSiDa=FaSiDaDa; So=BrSo=MoBrSo; Si=FaBrDa=MoSiDa. Some anthropologists find these algebraic equations are more convenient than diagrams for solving certain types of problems. Certainly the diagrams are clumsy, and substitutes for diagrams will be explored later. However, the diagrams remain widely used and are probably the clearest means for introducing the study of kinship.

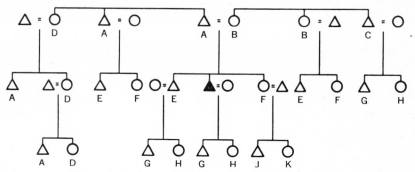

Figure O. Basic categories in Crow type terminology.

To return to the Crow system, you should be able to add many more relations now to the basic system of Figure O. Remember the rules of uniform descent and reciprocals. For your convenience the reciprocals from Figure O are the following pairs: A–G (approximates Fa-So), C–J (approximates MoBr-SiSo), E–E or E–F (approximates Br-Br or Br-Si).

EXERCISE 14 Supply the missing terms.

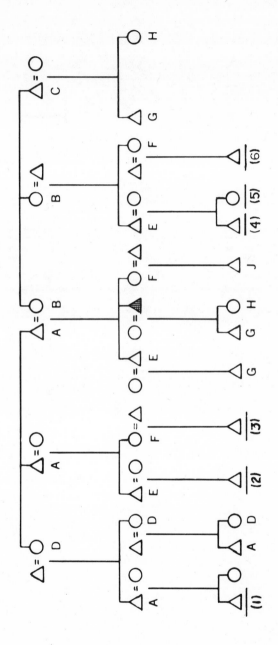

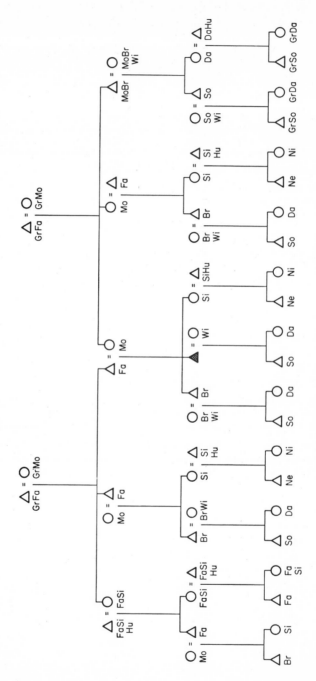

Figure P. Diagram of Crow terminology translated into English.

The diagram on p. 36 is provided with English terms instead of labeled categories in order to illustrate further how generational differences are overridden by the lineage principle. Remember that the use of English terms can be misleading, particularly in Crow, because each English term has a generation connotation that is absent in native words with Crow type terminology. The diagram reflects the nearest one can come in glossing a Crow system.

Behavior and Crow Terminology

So far, the terminology for a Crow system has been explained only in terms of a few logical principles. The terminology, however, is only a skeleton of the structure; the flesh of behavior is a necessary addition. Doubtless it is behavior that is most important for bringing a Crow system into being, although once in existence the relationship between terminology and behavior is much like skeleton and flesh. One cannot be explained as the cause of the other, but neither can be understood without reference to the other. A brief description of behavior patterns among some Trobriand relatives illustrates the essentials of a Crow system. Remember the basic characteristics: Ego has one kind of tie to his uterine (matrilineal) relatives, another kind of tie to his agnatic (patrilineal) relatives.

A full description of the behavior was first provided by Bronislaw Malinowski (1929); condensed versions may be found in Goldschmidt (1960: 233–299) or Fathauer (1961). Here the relationships are briefly paraphrased.

Trobrianders ignore the male's role in begetting children; the word for "father" carries only a social definition. As much as anything, it means "a man married to my mother." In some contexts a "father" is like a stranger or an outsider, but he is also like the American father who cares for his children and lavishes affection upon them. Unlike an American son, however, the maturing boy discovers he belongs to a group different from his father. He begins learning many duties, restrictions, and concerns for pride that unite him with his mother's group but necessarily separate him from father and his group.

As a boy matures the MoBr becomes a more important figure, and this male separates a boy even further from his father. The child begins to learn that he is regarded as a "stranger" in his father's village; his "own" or proper village is the one occupied by MoBr. In the village of MoBr a young man finds property rights, opportunity to succeed to office, and a future career. His natural allies and associates are the group associated with MoBr. In this circumstance, MoBr and his group increase authority over him, demand many services from him, and grant or withhold permission over a number of actions. Mother's brother will even determine in large measure whom ego will marry. Correspondingly, the authority and counsel of the father and his group decrease.

Perhaps the greatest difference between Trobrianders and Westerners is the link between mother and child. Recall the Trobriander belief that a mother contributes everything to the make up of the child. From this belief come the rules of inheritance, succession and rank, chieftainship, and magic. A man passes his position to his sister's son and this matrilineal link regulates marriage and restricts sex. The ideas of kinship are especially important at death. The norms specifying burial, mourning, distribution of food at the death feast, and other ritual are all based on the principle that matrilineal relatives form a special, closely knit group. The group is so tightly bound by common feelings and interests that even those united to it by marriage and by a father-to-child relation are sharply excluded in many ways. Crow terminology corresponds with these group distinctions, and terms mark off uterine relatives from agnatic relatives.

The Omaha Kinship System

The Omaha system of kinship terminology has been described as a mirror image of the Crow system. Both seem to develop from the same principles except that Omaha is based on patriliny. If the above exercises have provided a firm grasp of Crow terminology, then the following ones serve as a quick review of the principles. If you are still confused, it is well to review the Crow analysis quickly and then study the Omaha diagrams and exercises that follow.

To appreciate an Omaha system, return to the Washo hunters and gathers. If the Washo men adapted to herding domestic animals like cattle, the adaptation would bind men to a territory. A large number of males might cooperate in the herding; even more males, as a group, would defend the herds. Brothers and their sons could provide the basis for such a cooperating group; marriages would bring wives into this group. In such a case, residence is likely to become *patrilocal;* also described as *virilocal.* The wives, probably unrelated to each other, are married to men related consanguineally through descent. This *patrilineage* assumes the characteristics of a corporate group just as the previously described matrilineages of the Huron. Frequently the lineages form larger groupings as clans.

The strength of the patrilineage is reflected in the same way as the matrilineage in Crow systems. Indicate lineage membership and ego's relation to the lineages in the following exercise.

EXERCISE 15   Place a dot in the members of ego's lineage; place an X in the lineage members of ego's mother.

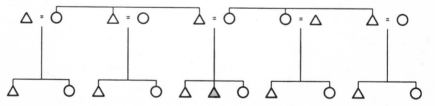

Remember that parallel uncles are in the same category as Fa. In Exercise 16 label members of this category "A". Parallel aunts are the same as mother. Label this group "B". Parallel cousins equate with brother and sisters. Label the males "C"; the females "D". Now think through ego's position with respect to his cross cousins. His matrilateral cross cousins (MoBrSo and MoBrDa) cannot be in his lineage, but they are lineage mates of his mother. MoBrSo is like a brother to mother; MoBrDa is like a sister—is a lineage sister—to mother. Therefore, MoBrSo is in the same category as MoBr. Label these two men as category "E." MoBrDa is in the same category as MoSi and mother. Extend the appropriate label to her. Now only the patrilateral cross cousins remain; their terms can be determined by the rule of reciprocity. Note in the diagram that ego equates his MoBrSo with MoBr; therefore, MoBrSo will equate ego with SiSo, the reciprocal for MoBr. Note in the exercise that the category, SiSo, is labeled "G." Since ego's FaSiSo is in this category, he will be labeled G. That is, G is the reciprocal of E.

EXERCISE 16   Categorize the following relatives according to Omaha type terminology. Repeat the exercise for the cross cousins, analyzing why one set of cross cousins is "elevated" a generation, the other set "lowered" a generation.

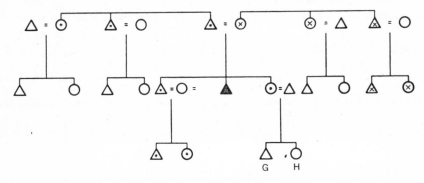

If the terms were translated into nearest English equivalents, the following terms would appear:

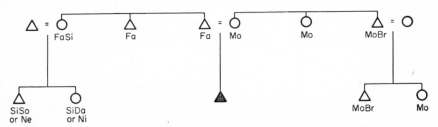

Figure Q. Nearest English terms for Omaha terminology.

Remember, however, that labeling the FaSiSo as a "nephew" is a distortion; what an Omaha system does is simply to equate the statuses of FaSiSo and SiSo.

One may note from Figure Q that Omaha terminology is a mirror image of Crow in that the patrilateral cousins have been "lowered" a generation while these are "raised" in Crow. The diagram has been made a mirror image, of course, by analyzing terminology in terms of English equivalents. Further, a complete reverse or mirror image should change male ego to female ego as in Figure R. Think now of ego's view of *her* matrilateral cross cousins. She is most likely to think in terms of MoBrDa who is equated with Mo. If she calls MoBrDa "mother"; then that woman will call her "daughter." That is, a FaSiDa is equated with "daughter." Thus, the patrilateral cross cousins become "daughter" and "son." Usually, but not always, the male speaking terms for patrilateral cross cousins differ from female speakers in Omaha system. Crow terms vary likewise.

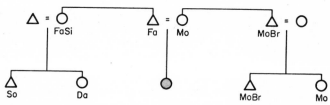

Figure R. Nearest English terms for Omaha terminology, female speaking.

The student should now be able to determine how the relatives two generations below ego will be grouped in both Crow and Omaha terminologies. In Exercise 17 complete the labeling or categorizing of relatives in an Omaha system.

EXERCISE 17 Label the relatives below ego's generation. Note that J and K have been provided as symbols for the "children" of an E. M is the symbol for children of J or K; M is also the symbol for children of G and H.

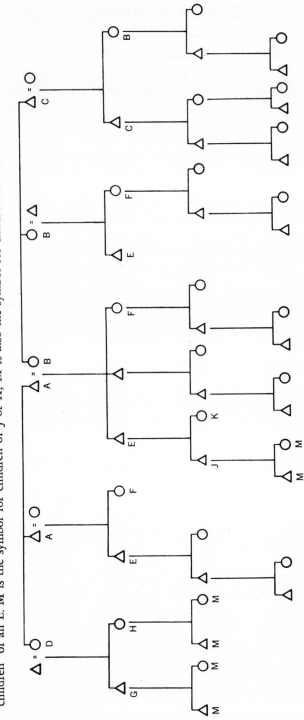

For a further understanding of Omaha terminology, it is useful to see how the principles apply in actual behavior. The Bunyoro provide an interesting example. In an ethnography written for students, Beattie (1960:48–60) describes concisely the relations between kin; his description is paraphrased here. It points up one view of why Omaha terms are what they are.

The Nyoro people are patrilineal, and an individual inherits his clan membership in a particular kin group and most of his property from his father. At one time all the men of a clan lived together, but now clans are somewhat scattered. The clans are exogamous and ideally patrilocal, but a number of factors other than descent now determine residence. Agnates, or patrilineal kinsmen, are still important in fixing personal loyalties, marriage, and inheritance; support and devotion among agnates are high. Thus, brothers usually reside near their fathers and keep close relations. This kind of *group* membership is stressed by Beattie; the social relations within the group greatly influence Nyoro thought about consaguine and affinal relatives and kinship terminology.

Nyoro terminology classifies some collateral relatives with lineal relatives. A FaBr is categorized with Fa, the FaBrSo is called the same as Br. A FaSi is called by a term that might be translated "female father." One's patrilateral relatives are either a kind of "sibling" or "fathers" (male and female), or children. To call them such, means to behave toward them largely as one does toward the nearest agnatic relatives. This usage extends to all persons within the clan, regardless of degree of relationship; furthermore, Nyoro consider it impolite to inquire about exact relationship between sib mates.

Relatives on the mother's side are also grouped together. MoSi is a kind of mother and her children are ego's siblings. The MoBr is a kind of "mother" and is called a "male mother." The practice seems strange, but remember that he is a member of the same lineage as mother. In a sense all the members of mother's agnatic group are "mothers."

The underlying principle is that members of one's own lineage are one kind of relative; members of mother's group are another kind of relative. Although Americans think of MoBr and FaBr as the same kind of relative and call both "uncle," the Nyoro see the two men as entirely different kinds of people. FaBr "belongs" to ego's important group; MoBr is only a member of mother's lineage. A Nyoro's expectations and obligations toward members of these two distinct groups are quite different.

A Nyoro is able to place almost anyone he meets in one of a few categories and immediately knows how he stands in relation to that person. If he meets a member of his own clan, that person is a father, brother, or son, depending on relative generation. Men of other clans may belong to mother's group, and therefore they become a kind of "mother"; or to FaMo clan and therefore a kind of "grandmother"; or to wife's clan and therefore a kind of brother-in-law. The clan system, combined with the classificatory principle, allows a few simple kin categories to be extended over a wide social field.

This system of kinship, which lends itself so well to Omaha terminology, consists of certain regular behavior between relatives. To contrast it with Crow organization, the relations between ego and his Fa, MoBr, and Mo will be described. Recall or review the behavior in these relationships for the Trobrianders.

A Nyoro father may have genuine affection for his son but the authority of fathers and the subordination of sons are always stressed. Fathers are addressed as "sir" or "master"; deference must be shown; and a man squats on the floor in the presence of his father. Fathers select a proper spouse for sons and prescribe when sons may begin to shave and smoke. The relation is marked by a latent hostility between the two. Beattie states that the son's rise to adulthood constitutes a challenge to the father and that a father resents his son's maturing because it threatens his own preeminence.

The relation to MoBr is much like that of a Trobriander for his father. Recall that the Nyoro MoBr is called a "male mother." This term is extended to MoBrSo and to the son of MoBrSo, which is the main characteristic of Omaha terminology. These relatives are all members of mother's agnatic descent group and so are categorized as "mother." A Nyoro thinks of himself as a child of the whole agnatic group and his kinship terms and behavior are based on this view. All the relatives that he calls "mother" are expected to be loving and indulgent. The "male mothers" are much the same as "mothers" and a sister's son is much freer with his MoBr's property than with his father's. He may borrow clothing, take food, and joke familiarly with MoBr. Nyoro often recount their happy visits to the homes of their maternal uncles.

For review, it is useful to compare carefully Trobriand and Nyoro behavior and analyze how this behavior accommodates itself so readily to Crow and Omaha kinship terminology. For further descriptions of behavior in patrilineal systems, see Faron (1968:22–56), Middleton (1965:25–42), Pospisil (1964: 37–46), Uchendu (1965:64–70); for matrilineal systems consult Dozier (1966: 39–57) and Lessa (1966:16–30).

The Causes of Crow and Omaha Terminology

Crow and Omaha systems are of particular interest to anthropologists partly because they are so different from more familiar systems. More importantly, the two clearly reveal that factors other than sex, generation, or consanguinity—factors with a biological base—account for kinship terms. Radcliffe-Brown's explanation that a "lineage principle" overrides a "generation principle" is not a complete explanation but it does demonstrate that sociological institutions are also factors in kinship. A high correlation between patrilineages and Omaha types, and matrilineages and Crow types is proof of the importance of a sociological cause. However, a society may have patrilineages without Omaha terms, or matrilineages without Crow terminology. Furthermore, a few societies have Crow or Omaha terminology while lacking lineages. Lounsbury (1964:354) even reports that five societies have Crow terminology in association with patrilineal kin groupings. Sociological factors can be considered only one of the causes of kinship, a point well made by Lounsbury.

Another factor must be the influence of neighboring groups. Diffusion and borrowing were once used as primary explanations for why peoples had the terminology they have. Few anthropologists now would accept such a view. However, peoples next to each other do tend to have similar systems, and a culture area frequently may be characterized by one of the systems. On the other hand, in a few places all the different kinds of terminologies occur in one restricted area. In these culture areas it would appear that each group independently invented its own system, but such an analysis is as extreme as attributing everything to diffusion.

The variation in distribution of kin types has led some anthropologists to argue that particular kinship systems can be understood only through their histories. That is, a number of complex historical events must account for the similarities between systems that are widely separated with very different individual histories.

Sol Tax (1955a) resolves these problems in an analysis of one area with a variety of kin types. He shows how it is misleading to argue on the basis of sociological versus psychological, diffusion versus independent invention, or historical versus natural law. Actually all factors may be important and the task of the anthropologist is to identify the contribution of each. Moreover, it is often difficult to put a kinship terminological system in either a cause or effect relationship with institutions such as lineages and marriage practices.

In short the analysis of kinship is a complex operation, and the student should realize that the explanations and exercises presented so far have been accompanied by simple, monocausal arguments. These explanations were only for the purpose of giving *an understanding of the total system.* One must first comprehend the system *as a total system,* then proceed to look for full explanation. A complete understanding of why kinship systems are what they are is far off, but one cannot begin to analyze them without first knowing how they may be classified. Of course, the classifications are not an end in themselves; they do not have explanatory power. Classifications, however, are generally clues to processes both in forming cognitive categories and in forming social groups.

Review of Classification by Cousin Terminology

Westerners seldom find difficulty with the Eskimo, Hawaiian, and Sudanese systems. Eskimo equates all patrilateral cousins with all matrilateral cousins and differentiates them from siblings. Hawaiian equates all cousins with siblings; there are no cousin terms. A Sudanese system has different terms for each type of cousin and sibling. A major characteristic of these systems is that the matrilateral relatives are treated much like the patrilateral relatives; commonly descent is simply bilateral. It is possible to have descent groups, but the descent may pass through either sex. Such groups, generally described as nonunilineal descent groups, will be discussed later in Part Two.

The other three kinship systems are usually associated with unilineal descent. The Iroquois system equates parallel cousins with siblings while distinguishing cross cousins. Crow and Omaha systems essentially make the same distinctions but instead of having a special category of cross cousins, these statuses are raised or lowered a generation. In Crow systems the patrilateral cousins are raised, FaSiSo=

Fa, FaSiDa=FaSi; and the matrilateral cousins are lowered, MoBrSo=So, MoBrDa=Da. In Omaha systems the matrilateral cousins are raised, MoBrSo= MoBr, MoBrDa=Mo; and the patrilateral cousins are lowered, FaSiSo=Ne, FaSiDa=Ni.

Remember that this classification is based on terminology for *cousins*. One expects certain terms for parent's siblings given certain cousin terms. For example Iroquois terms for cousins would indicate bifurcate merging terms for first ascending generation. However, such consistency does not always occur. This type of inconsistency is almost surely a result of culture change (Service 1962:139). A new classification that takes into account terms for both the first ascending and ego's same generation is necessary. Dole (1969) states the problem clearly and offers "bifurcate generation" for a kinship nomenclature, with Hawaiian cousin terms and bifurcate merging terms for parent's siblings. A new classification system, like Dole's, will be helpful for the study of culture change, but recall that taxonomy is only a means to an end. A proliferation of classifications would make kinship analysis just a sophisticated form of butterfly collecting. Indeed Leach (1961) suggests that many anthropologists have already become such collectors.

General Review

A basic vocabulary for kinship study has been introduced in this first part. It is essential for further work that this vocabulary be mastered. Write out definitions for the following terms. Answers may be checked with the glossary.

consanguineal

affinal

pseudo relation

family of orientation

family of procreation

reference, term of

address, term of

sororate

levirate

parallel cousins

cross cousins

lineage

sib

clan

patrilineal descent

agnate

matrilineal descent

bilateral descent

endogamy

exogamy

The major point of Part One is meant to train students in classifying kinship systems on the basis of terminology. Classify the following systems by cousin and first ascending generation typologies. The terminologies are those of particular cultures; usually it is possible to construct limited charts like these from an early dictionary prepared by a nonanthropologist.

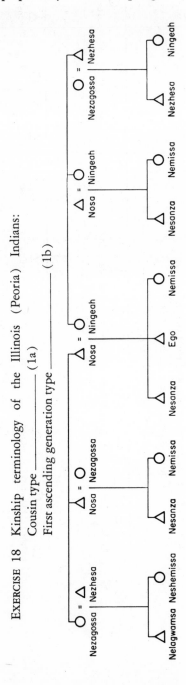

EXERCISE 18   Kinship terminology of the Illinois (Peoria) Indians:

Cousin type _____ (1a)

First ascending generation type _____ (1b)

EXERCISE 19 Kinship terminology of the Dakota Indians:

Cousin type ——————— (2a)

First ascending generation type ——————— (2b)

EXERCISE 20   Kinship terminology of a Javanese village:

Cousin type ——————— (3a)

First ascending generation type ——————— (3b)

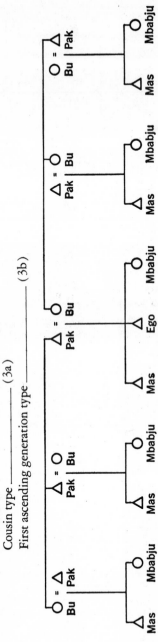

EXERCISE 21   Kinship terminology of a North American tribe:

Cousin type ——————— (4a)

First ascending generation type ——————— (4b)

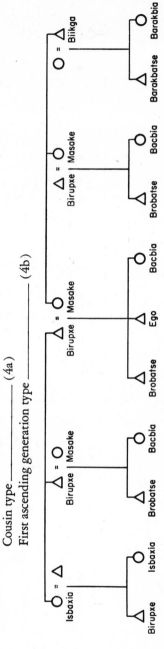

PART TWO

ANALYSIS
OF KINSHIP BEHAVIOR

Collecting Kinship Terms

THE PRECEDING CHAPTER indicated the importance of collecting kinship terms from both sexes. In some societies few differences for male or female speakers will be found; in other societies the terminology for men is very different from women. Anthropologists have not provided much information on the actual details of collecting terminology from informants, although Williams (1967) and others are helping to rectify this situation. In the field, ethnographers talk to as many people as they can, hopefully collecting a representative sample. The informants are asked about all their relatives. In some societies deceased ancestors are among the first discussed; elsewhere the mention of dead relatives may be avoided. Such relatives must be determined in roundabout ways. Eventually genealogies are collected for numerous individuals; in small communities the relationship of every person may be determined. (For recording the kin ties for about one hundred families of a Dakota community, I resorted to using thirty feet of butcher's wrapping paper. However, genealogies of particular adults can usually be recorded on an 8 by 11 sheet.) Presently anthropologists are experimenting with computers which may be used to record and display the genealogical map of a community.

The fieldworker soon discovers that any one person lacks certain types of relatives. An informant may not have a MoBr, but gaps in the terminology are filled in by additional informants. This method is highly reliable for establishing the terms used. Since most people like to talk and gossip about relatives, the fieldworker is soon into many areas of behavior. It is, of course, the behavior that is most important and eventually must be fully documented. Nowhere is the behavior of kin better described than in Chagnon (1968:54–81), and this monograph is highly recommended as a study of kinship.

It is a good, initial exercise for the student to collect several genealogies from one's friends. These data may be compared with the genealogy of a Dakota Indian, one of the author's informants, in Figure S. Although this informant seems to have many relatives (note that his affines are not even shown), he lacks several significant relations. In this case ego would not provide terms for MoBr or MoSi because his mother was a sole surviving child. Therefore, matrilateral parallel and cross cousins are missing. Further, Dakota have different terms for older and younger brother; here ego is the youngest sibling and would employ only the older brother term.

Obviously, however, ego knows the term for younger brother because his older brothers use it in speaking to him. Likewise, he has heard other Dakota use terms for MoBr and MoSi. Thus, informants are able to complete a hypothetical kinship chart with all possible relatives included as well as concrete genealogies. Lewis Morgan, described by Eggan (1960, 1966) as the pioneer of kinship studies, simply used a list of over 100 items and collected kinship terms much as one would compile a dictionary.

The genealogical method should be combined with the hypothetical method; it is particularly more revealing where societies are undergoing change. Generally, collecting genealogies also provides the best access to much of community life.

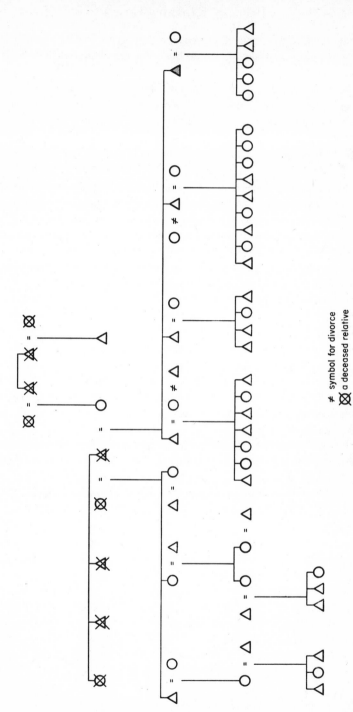

≠ symbol for divorce
⊠ a deceased relative

Figure 5. The genealogy of a Dakota Indian

nformants are almost always ready to talk about their actual relatives either praising or disparaging them. In fact, gossip is derived from an old English kinship term *godsib* (Mintz and Wolf 1950). For very short periods of research, as a check on genealogies, or for some work involving only terminology, the hypothetical method may suffice.

However, in most cases a wide sample is essential. Informants vary widely in their ability to understand what the ethnographer wants to know. Some individuals, particularly the elderly, may immediately comprehend what is involved in kinship (I have seen some Dakota begin drawing their own diagrams), whereas others have great difficulty in extending terminology beyond actual relatives. Under conditions of culture change a wide sample also will provide former as well as new terms.

Indeed the analysis of changing kinship systems is itself a subject. Bruner (1955), Eggan (1937), and Spoehr (1947) provide data on changing Crow systems; their work is a foundation for empirical studies such as Lange's description of Cochiti (1959:367–396, 1967). Murdock (1949) presents some logical sequences that kinship systems could be expected to follow, and these sequences have been demonstrated among a few groups (Voget, 1953). Service (1962) and Dole (1960) interpret changing kinship systems in terms of evolutionary theory; Dole (1969) has presented a convincing, empirical case of one evolutionary sequence among the Kuikuru.

At this point it is useful to recall the Australians who needed to know their relationship to one another in order to begin any interaction. Once they recognize kin status relations to each other, they have defined the other in terms of themselves. In short the terms are a kind of index for behavior or a map of perception. Generally it is behavior that is the subject of analysis. Most behavior will be kin based, and terminology is a key to analyzing the behavior, but the terms are also an index of how people think. Kin terms indicate groups of statuses. Study of the meanings of the terms may reveal patterns of cognition or the way people form categories.

The Analysis of Meaning in Terminology

From a wide-ranging knowledge of kinship terminologies, A. L. Kroeber (1909) deduced eight criteria that appeared to be used in various combinations by the world's cultures to create kin groupings. These criteria were: 1) different or same generation, 2) lineal or collateral relation, 3) relative age within same generation, 4) sex of relative, 5) sex of speaker, 6) sex of person who is a link between one relative and another, 7) consanguine or affinal, 8) whether a linking relative is dead or alive. Not all peoples use all the criteria; any system employs them in different combinations. Kroeber's insight was so keen that little change has been made in his list. Murdock (1949) added a criteria of "polarity" but other than that the list was virtually unaltered for sixty years. Goodenough (1970) has qualified these criteria further and added much understanding from his own far-reaching knowledge of kinship systems. Goodenough (1970:88) drops Murdock's

criteria of polarity and adds three new criteria. This limited modification testifies
to the remarkable insight of Kroeber.

Goodenough's contribution stems from his own work (1956*b*) and that of
Lounsbury (1956). Basically, they developed a methodology that would indicate
how these criteria are used for forming classes or groups of relatives. The method
is called *componential analysis* and is much like the *formal analysis* devised by
linguists in semantic analysis. Goodenough (1970:72), for instance, defines componential analysis as "a method for forming and testing hypotheses about what
words signify." Romney (1965:127) suggests that componential analysis is analo-
gous to phonemic analysis. It reduces the redundancy of a transcription; that is, by
indicating the meaning of terms in the most economical or parsimonious manner,
the rules of the system may be best understood.

Initially the procedure relied heavily upon the abbreviations introduced
early in this text. Analysists soon saw that other notational systems were not only
shorter but clearer. Before considering these shorthand devices, give further thought
to Kroeber's criteria as seen in English terms. What criteria are in the term brother?
That is, what is the *meaning* of brother? What does the term tell you about the
person?

First, of course, it tells you that the person is a *relative*, the word is a
kinship term. Furthermore a brother is 1) of same generation, 4) a male, 7) a
consanguine. What are the components of aunt? An aunt is 1) of different
generation, 2) a collateral relative, 4) a female. Unlike "brother" she may be
an affinal or consanguine relative. In English some criteria seem very important:
Generation is indicated in all terms; even specific generations are indicated by the
prefix "great." In other systems, other criteria may underlie the terms. The criteria
of life or death of linking relative and sex of linking relative are not known in
English, but they occur in many other societies.

The problem, therefore, is to develop a systematic method for determining
the criteria that are employed. The methodology should reveal what an English
speaker more or less intuitively "knows" about his terms. Assume that you are a
Hopi Indian anthropologist trying to determine the meaning of aunt, as used by an
English speaker. Your raw data would be reduced initially to the following form:

"aunt"	=	MoSi		MZ
		MoBrWi	or	MBW
		FaSi		FZ
		FaBrWi		FBW

Probably your first conclusion is that "femaleness" is one criterion. The immediate
check is: Are there any males called "aunt"? If not, sex of relative must be a component of the term. How soon would you, as a Hopi, see that all these women are a
generation above ego? The check is: Are any aunts in the same generation or a
generation below ego? After you concluded "aunt" was one generation above ego
would it not be confirming evidence to find that "great-aunts" were women two
generations above ego? How long would you puzzle over whether aunts were
consanguine or affinal relatives? If you had asked an English speaker, "Is your aunt

a blood relative?" he may well have answered "yes," and most other English terms do indicate affinity or consanguinity. Furthermore, if you only observed English speakers closely, you might have concluded that life or death of a linking relative must be a component. When a FaBr dies, ego is likely to lose touch with his widow. The usual kin behavior may disappear. But upon pursuing the question (as a good anthropologist) most informants will maintain that FaBrWi is still an "aunt." Obviously, a methodology that will insure analysis of the criteria employed in kinship terminologies is essential.

Hopefully, you are beginning to appreciate the problems in determining components of kinship terms and will accept notational systems that simplify the data. In componential analysis a compromise is needed for a string of primary kin terms, such as MoBrWi, and a kinship chart that is confusing because it contains extraneous relations. For instance, in analyzing the meaning of "aunt," a Hopi anthropologist would record:

$$aunt \ = \ \begin{aligned} &MZ \\ &MBW \\ &FZ \\ &FBW \end{aligned}$$

He would have noted that both male and female speakers use the term in the same ways. He could chart these relations somewhat differently using "m" for male and "f" for female and "x" for sex where sex is not a criterion. A single line indicates consanguinity; a double line affinity; and relative position indicates generation. For instance:

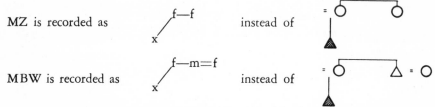

At this point formula-like phrases simply have been substituted for abbreviations (for example, MZ) and no simplification has occurred. Note above that the criteria of generation and consanguinity or affinity are expressed in the traditional way while the Mars and Venus symbols have been replaced by m (male) and f (female).

Simplification can be achieved by letting "x" equal either sex.

MZ would be f—f / x

FZ would be m—f / x   simplified to   x—f / x

Further reduction in the expression follows with:

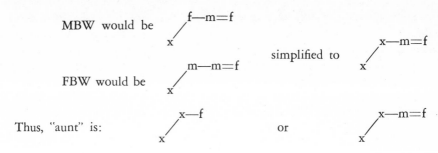

The two expressions are not only more economical than the four strings of primary kin terms but also make it immediately apparent that the term includes both criteria of affinity and consanguinity.

However, you are likely unimpressed with the economy and you doubt that it would be too difficult to determine that "aunts" are affines as well as consanguineals. Perhaps you will appreciate the notational system much more if you use it for analysis of some esoteric terms. Among Kalmuk Mongols the term, *tor'l–tor'l*, occurs as a common reciprocal term. (Like the English reciprocal, "cousin-cousin," it includes many different relatives.) The traditional notation would list the following meanings for *tor'l*:

tor'l =	Fa	FaFaFa	FaFaFaSoDa
	Mo	FaFaMo	FaFaFaSoSo
	So	SoSoDa	FaFaSoSoDa
	Da	SoSoSo	FaFaSoSoSo
	FaFa	FaFaSoSo	FaFaFaDa
	FaMo	FaFaSoDa	FaFaFaSo
	SoSo	FaFaFaSoSoDa.	FaSoSoDa
	SoDa	FaFaFaSoSoSo	FaSoSoSo

What do you see in this listing that all the terms have in common? That is, what are the criteria for *tor'l* as a kinship term? When the above terms are converted to the new notational system, note not only the reduction, but also the clarification.

The first four terms, Fa, Mo, So, Da, can all be expressed simply as:

$$\begin{array}{c} x \\ | \\ x \end{array}$$

All the kin strings can be expressed as:

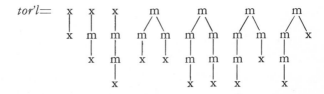

The twenty-four abbreviated terms are reduced to seven expressions. Most importantly, one is led to an immediate hypothesis: *Tor'l* is a reciprocal between kin where there are no female linking relatives.

Since English speakers do not use this criterion, sex of linking relative, in their kinship, it is difficult for them to see any principle accounting for the grouping represented by the twenty-four abbreviations. But in the notational system, the lack of any f (female) links is immediately apparent.

Another new notational system substitutes plus and minus signs for relative placement to indicate generation. Romney (1965:129) describes it at length. Briefly, the system is:

m	represents male
f	represents female
a	represents person of either sex
=	represents marriage bond
O	represents sibling link
+	represents parent link
—	represents child link

In this system ego is represented by the first symbol; the relative he is referring to by the last. The final symbol might also be called the *alter ego*. Consider how aunt could be expressed:

MoSi is $a + f \, O \, f$. FaSi is $a + m \, O \, f$. The one phrase, $a + a \, O \, f$, may be substituted for both. MoBrWi is $a + f \, O \, m = f$. FaBrWi is $a + m \, O \, m = f$. These phrases reduce to: $a + a \, O \, m = f$.

The traditional and new notational systems can be depicted as:

aunt = MoSi   x—f
           FaSi   x $a + a \, O \, f$

           MoBrWi   x—m = f
           FaBrWi   x $a + a \, O \, m = f$

The latter notational system presently appears to be the most widely used for componential analysis. Romney (1965) provides a set of rules for reducing these algebraic-like expressions to their simplest form as well as rules for expanding the basic form to generate the original system. The method is closely linked to new developments in linguistics; in fact, the basic work, by Lounsbury (1956) and Goodenough (1956b), first appeared in a linguistics journal.

For the purposes of this text, it is sufficient simply to understand the notational systems; use of the notations is a foundation for final analysis.

EXERCISE 22 Write the traditional notation for the English term, "grand-mother" and express the relationship with each of the new notation systems.

Grandmother =

Another system of charting relationships is popular because it readily demonstrates three dimensions or three criteria. The system is appropriate for English terms, which basically consist of three components, and students will likely encounter this kind of analysis of English. Modifications of the chart resulting from application of this system are often applied to other terminologies.

TABLE 2

A MODIFICATION OF WALLACE AND ATKINS (1960) IDENTIFICATION OF DIMENSIONS IN ENGLISH TERMINOLOGY

Dimension A is sex of relative. A1 is male. A2 is female.
Dimension B is generation. $+1$ a generation above ego; 0 same generation; -1 a generation below ego.
Dimension C is lineality. C1 is lineal; C2 is collateral.

| | C1 | | C2 | | |
	A1	A2	A1	A2	
$+2$	Grandfather	Grandmother	Great Uncle	Great Aunt	(?) Cousin once removed
$+1$	Father	Mother	Uncle	Aunt	
0	Ego		Brother	Sister	Cousin
-1	Son	Daughter	Nephew	Niece	Cousin once removed
-2	Grandson	Granddaughter	Great Nephew	Grand Niece	(?)

For the final steps in a componential analysis of English terminology, the student may consult Wallace and Atkins (1960). Buchler and Selby (1968:181–190) provide an alternative analysis of the English.

The usefulness of such diagramming can also be illustrated by an analysis of Cibecue Apache made by Basso. He reports terms that are of Iroquois type for cousins but are an unusual type for the first ascending generation. Therefore, the use of the traditional types of classification is inadequate for reporting the terminology. Basso (1970:12) summarizes his data in the following ,manner:

Gen + 1	šima	šita	šima?a	šit?a	šibeže
	Mo	Fa	MoSi	MoBr	FaSi; FaBr

Gen 0	šila	šikisn	šila?aš	šizege
	Si; FaBrDa MoSiDa	Br; FaBrSo MoSiSo	FaSiSo; MoBrSo	FaSiDa; MoBrDa

Landar (1962) and Burling (1963) provide analyses of still other terminologies while a special issue of the *American Anthropologist* (Vol. 67, No. 5, Part 2) explores the subject in depth. Burling (1964) has written a penetrating critique of componential analysis suggesting its use is limited. On the other hand, Selby (1970) sees the method as part of an entirely new theoretical approach in anthropology.

Behavior and Kinship

In many different parts of the world similar, institutionalized behavior is found between sets of relatives. The behavior ranges from one of extreme respect to a rough, slapstick kind of joking. The type of behavior indicates the nature of the relationship between statuses or groups.

Avoidance is an extreme form of respect. The Navajo are well known for their custom of avoiding their mother-in-law. When a man approaches the hogan or house of his mother-in-law, he may cough or laugh loudly; his mother-in-law responds to this cue by leaving. Or a man may postpone his visit if he knows his mother-in-law is present. Mother-in-law bell earrings have become a popular tourist item in the Southwest. A good son-in-law is warned by the tone of his mother-in-law's earrings and leaves before she arrives. Opler (1947) provides a number of cases illustrating avoidance among the Apache. More often a *respect relation* does not require avoidance but simple circumspect behavior. Commonly it is between generations; most often it occurs between brother and sister. Some cases of avoidance have even been reported for brother–sister but simple respect is to be expected. The respect relationship occurs between relatives who frequently interact but who inherently have conflicting interests. The conflicting interests between a brother and sister are usually their spouses. The affect toward a husband may well distract a woman from her prescribed duties for a brother.

A mild *joking relation* complements respect. Generally more distant relatives are involved, but in some cultures brothers regularly joke with each other. Frequently grandparents and grandchildren are expected to joke with each other because grandparents exert no authority over grandchildren. In Western societies the relationship combines a lack of restraint with some teasing, but a general age respect prevents an institutionalized joking relation so frequently found elsewhere.

At the opposite extreme from avoidance is an *obligatory joking relation*. Radcliffe-Brown called it "permitted disrespect." The relationship is essentially friendly but with potential hostility. Siblings-in-law are most often in an obligatory joking relation and the joking assumes sexual, practical, or satirical forms. Robert

Lowie (1935:28) reports an example of obligatory joking that illustrates the structure of these institutionalized relations.

> A Crow Indian is on terms of the greatest familiarity with his own brother's or clansman's wife. Similarly, he may treat his wife's sister with the utmost license, e.g., raising her dress as to expose her nakedness; and she may jest with him in corresponding fashion. In 1916 I spent a good deal of time in the camp of one informant who was forever fondling and teasing his wife's younger sister, while she returned his treatment in kind. They were not the least embarrassed by the wife's or my presence nor by that of an adult son by a previous marriage of the man's.

The factors accounting for structured behavior must be similar to those for kinship terminology. Some of the explanations for this patterned behavior provide important insights into kinship. Radcliffe-Brown's early analysis (1952: 109–10) of respect and joking centered on the structure of society. He believed that where dual organizations were sharply separated but regularly interconnected by marriage, institutionalized behavior would occur. That is, relationships that were marked by both detachment and attachment led to forms of avoidance or joking.

Fred Eggan (1955:79) further refined the analysis of patterned kinship behavior. He developed a number of hypotheses to explain which type of behavior would occur with particular relationships.

> *Respect relationship*—where there is some possibility of conflict and the social necessity for avoiding it.
> *Mild joking relationship*—where there is some possibility of conflict but no particular social necessity for avoiding it.
> *Avoidance relationship*—where the conflict situation is inevitable, where there is the social necessity of avoiding it, and where generation differences are present.
> *Obligatory joking relationship*—where the conflict situation is inevitable, where there is the social necessity of avoiding it, but where no differences of generation are involved.

Although the patterned relations are usually reciprocal, each partner joking equally, an asymmetrical relationship may occur. A sister's son, for instance, may tease or embarrass his mother's brother while the latter may not retaliate. Anthropologists need to explore further this nonreciprocal form; nor is the field of structured kinship behavior as well understood as it should be.

Marriage and Kinship

Like patterned kin behavior, marriage customs are closely related to kinship. The sororate and levirate are prime examples; likewise, endogamy and exogamy (see glossary) are based on kinship. In Western society there are no good examples of exogamy; marriage out of the nuclear family follows incest regulations not an exogamous rule. Westerners do tend to be endogamous within social class, race, and major religion, but the practice has little to do with kinship. Elsewhere, however, the rules may regualte marriage between parallel or cross cousins or most likely some other category of relative.

When an anthropologist today correlates marriage customs and kinship practices, he hesitates to define any causal relation between the two. Early anthropologists, like Lewis H. Morgan, tried to demonstrate that marriage practices had "caused" many types of families and terminologies. These early explanations were soon shown to be wrong, but it became clear that marriage was an important aspect of kinship. Therefore, some knowledge of marriage customs is necessary for any analysis of kinship.

a. *Marriage as a rite of passage.*

The significant changes in status between birth and death are termed *rites de passage* (Van Gennep, 1908). Birth, puberty, marriage, and death are marked off with ritual events by almost all societies. Marriage, as a rite of passage, involves a change in status from single to married and often from carefree youth to responsible adult. Furthermore, it means that an individual acquires a new set of relatives and must learn new relationships. Probably of greatest importance, marriage is an arrangement between groups that symbolizes a special alliance between them. For the individual, marriage is dangerous because of many new status relations; groups are concerned about the marriage as an affirmation of existing relations. Therefore, marriage is generally surrounded by supernatural supports and a multitude of norms to serve as guidelines.

b. *Marriage and children.*

Marriage in many places emphasizes the procreation of children. Modern Western concepts of marriage differ so radically from this attitude that the importance of children in other societies must be noted. Where such an attitude prevails, one better understands a practice such as *trial marriage.* In trial marriage a couple live together long enough to determine if they can bear children. Only after a birth is the marriage complete.

c. *Number of spouses.*

In Western society norms prescribing *monogamy* are so strong that one often considers multiple spouses as somehow "unnatural." However, a theme of multiple spouses occurs in Western literature and students show unusual interest in *polygamous* systems. Polygamy takes two forms. *Polygyny* consists of multiple wives; *polyandry* consists of multiple husbands. Although many Hollywood personalities experience more than one spouse, they can be married to only one at a time. This practice is termed *serial monogamy.* It is found in a few societies other than our own. Polyandry is rare; polygyny fairly common. In fact, in terms of numbers of cultures polygyny occurs more often than monogamy (Murdock, 1957:686).

d. *Attitudes toward affines.*

As noted before, the advantages of marriage are balanced by the difficulties of new relationships. The reluctance to assume such status relations is epitomized by a practice of *bride capture* where the bride and her relatives perform mock combat before she is carried off by the groom and his relatives. Hesitation about marriage seems largely to stem from recognition that one will acquire a host of new relatives, one's affines. The problem of new relatives is reduced partially through the levirate; the problem is solved even more neatly by marrying a cousin. Ego's father-in-law and mother-in-law are already his uncle and aunt. With cross cousin marriage even terms for in-laws may be absent. This type of marriage occurs in so many cultures in so many different parts of the world that it must have great functional value, although it is not fully understood. Cousin marriage has so many ramifications on kinship that it will be treated separately in the next section.

e. *Acquiring a spouse.*

Almost everywhere marriage involves a transfer of wealth as well as women. Westerners are familiar with a *dowry* and generally think of it as the bride's family giving wealth to the groom. Actually the dowry may be better understood as a woman's share of her father's estate. Possibly more significant in Western marriage is the groom's gift of the wedding ring. It symbolizes the husband's group giving wealth to the bride's family. Such a transfer is the common custom among the world's peoples. This *bride wealth* may be in the form of iron as well as gold or even cattle or pigs. Whatever the form, it is largely symbolic and the iron or cows cannot be equated with currency. Unfortunately many missionaries and colonial officials did make such an equation and concluded that many Africans and Asians purchased their wives as if they were chattel. In fact the bride wealth often insures that the wife will be well treated; more importantly the bride wealth generally determines the lineage membership of children. To emphasize the point some anthropologists use the term *progeny wealth* rather than bride wealth. *Bride service* may substitute for bride wealth; a man works for his father-in-law or the bride's lineage. The practice results in a mixture of initial matrilocal residence followed by patrilocal residence. Finally some societies forego economic exchange by making a direct, reciprocal exchange of sisters. In *sister exchange* marriage a man says in effect, "I will give you my sister as a bride if you will give me your sister." (Recall that in most kinship systems there are many women in the category of sister.) If this custom is institutionalized, the web of relationships becomes complex and soon much more involved than a trade between two men.

Cousin Marriages

When sister exchange is practiced over two or more generations, it may also be viewed as the marriage of cross cousins. Earlier anthropologists explained quite simply that sister exchange caused cross cousin marriage. Again contemporary anthropologists are cautious in providing such a causal explanation. What can be said is that sister exchange is intrinsically related to cross cousin marriage. The point is well made by diagraming the practice.

EXERCISE 23 Diagram sister exchange practiced over three generations.

Consider carefully the simplified diagram provided as an answer at the back. Then ask yourself the following: Why are all the marriages always between cross cousins and never parallel cousins? How is ego related to his mother-in-law and daughter-in-law or other affines? If ego is in a patrilineage, what will be his ties to his mother's lineage?

The diagram should clarify how sister exchange and cross cousin marriage are simply two aspects of one system. Of course not every marriage in a group must conform to the norm, and a "proper" exchange need involve only women who are in a category of sister to the men involved. Indeed, most cross cousin marriages are not with an actual cross cousin but with someone in the same category. Remember that most terminologies categorize parallel cousins with sisters; moreover, cross cousin marriage puts all parallel cousins in ego's lineage. Lineages are exogamous, so only cross cousins are eligible spouses.

Remember further that the functional value of cross cousin marriage is not completely understood. The person who has troubles with his own in-laws will appreciate the psychological explanation that in-laws are "eliminated." That is, ego's mother-in-law was his FaSi and his MoBrWi before his marriage. From birth he had learned to interact with her. Well-established personal relationships ame-liorate many problems in status changes that marriage brings.

However, it seems unlikely that a social system would be planned to eliminate in-laws in such a way. Instead the major functional value of cross cousin marriage appears to lie in the way it consistently links major groups. Where lineages are a major part of the social structure, a society tends toward vertical splitting or fissioning; that is, an individual's loyality and obligations toward his lineage tend to produce conflict with other lineages within the society. Lineage exogamy means marriages will link lineages in horizontal fashion, but where members of lineage P marry members of all other lineages then the horizontal ties are weak ones. Cross cousin marriage, however, provides many consistent ties with one lineage; lineage P members marry only Q members. The custom firmly unites two lineages and reduces the number of cleavages by half. Of course, like all human groupings, the fusion of P and Q and then X and Y means an increased difference between group (PQ) and group (XY).

EXERCISE 24 To make sure you understand cross cousin marriage and lineage alliance, place a dot in the members of ego's patrilineage, a cross in the patrilineage of ego's wife.

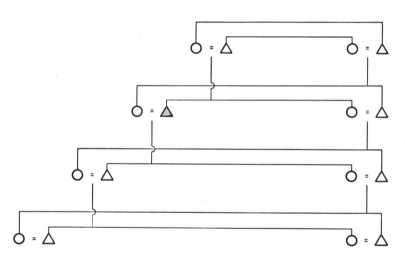

The system diagrammed shows the effects of *bilateral cross cousin* marriage. Ego is marrying not only his MoBrDa but also his FaSiDa. Of course no society could manage for all its members to marry in such a way. Nor do many societies even have such a norm. What many do have, however, is regular exchange of women between two major groupings that very much resembles bilateral cross cousin marriage. Ego selects a spouse from the category of women that includes MoBrDa and FaSiDa.

Although rare, marriage may also occur with a parallel cousin. Murphy and Kasdan (1959) describe the practice in the Moslem world. The subject is over-shadowed by cross cousin analysis. Of even more interest to anthropologists has been a practice that prescribes marriage with only one of the cross cousins.

Unilateral Cross Cousin Marriage

A few societies have managed an exchange of women in such a regular, predictable way that a model of their social structure would seem to have required complex engineering. Through a norm that directs marriage for a man with only one of his cousins, lineages seem to become equally and regularly linked. In effect, lineage P gives its women to Q who give to R who give to P. When ego marries only the MoBrDa, the system is called *matrilateral cross cousin marriage*; marriage with FaSiDa is termed *patrilateral cross cousin marriage*. The two systems are described as *asymmetric* in contrast to the *symmetric* form of bilateral cross cousin marriage.

Figure T diagrams the two asymmetric systems. Note that a group stands as wife-givers to one group and wife-takers to another group. Further note that in matrilateral cross cousin marriage, women from one lineage are always given in marriage to men of the same second lineage. In patrilateral cross cousin marriage a lineage gives women to a second lineage in one generation and then receives women from that second lineage in the next generation. Finally note that the exchange will be the same regardless of whether the groups are matrilineal or patrilineal.

Figure T. Unilateral cross cousin marriage.

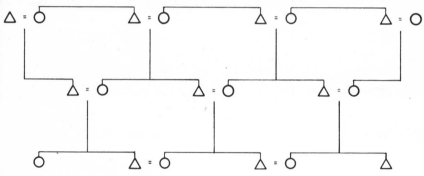

Matrilateral cross cousin marriage

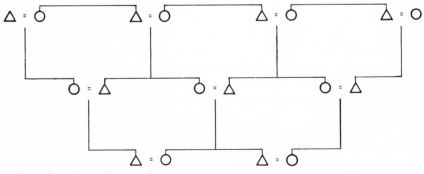

Patrilateral cross cousin marriage

Unilateral cross cousin marriage long puzzled anthropologists who concen trated on the symmetric form instead. Finally, Claude Levi-Strauss (1949) ex plained in depth why matrilateral cross cousin marriage was more prevalent than patrilateral cross cousin marriage. Josselin de Jong (1952) brought Levi-Strauss' French work to the attention of many English readers. Homans and Schneide. (1955) recognized its great theoretical importance but offered a different inter pretation. In turn, their views were criticized at length by Needham (1962a) who defended Levi-Strauss. Some anthropologists feel the controversy has gotten out o' hand; certainly, it has been one of the most written about issues in social anthro pology. Very briefly Levi-Strauss maintains that matrilateral cross cousin marriage promotes greater social solidarity because wife-givers and wife-takers regularly stand in the same relationship. With patrilateral cross cousin marriage these stand ings reverse themselves every generation and relationships cannot be as stable Homans and Schneider contend that the matrilateral form is three times as preva lent as the patrilateral form because patrilineal descent groups outnumber matri lineal descent groups. In patrilineal groups the father will stand as an authoritative figure while the MoBr will be warm and indulgent. The sentiments toward the MoBr will be extended to his daughter, who then becomes ego's wife.

The student who wishes to pursue the issue in depth may start with: Need ham (1958, 1960, 1961), Livingstone (1959), Berting and Philipsen (1960) Eyde and Postal (1961), Coult (1962a, 1962b), Lane (1962), Ackerman (1964) and Spiro (1964). Schneider (1963) links the controversy with another majo debate, one over the relative importance of marriage and descent (Fortes 1959) (Leach 1957).

Sections and Subsections

Before the analysis of unilateral cross cousin marriage, complex linkages through marriage were seen in Australian practices. The analysis of how these systems worked has also been controversial. Rather than examine the controversy in depth, it is more useful here to see how marriage norms, combined with other rules can produce an intricate web of relationships. Among many Australian tribes a four-way link establishes most status relations. In effect, a man of group W marries a woman of group X; their children are members of group Y who must marry into group Z. These groupings are known as *sections* or sometimes *classes*. A few Australian tribes have compounded the differences with subsections, creating eight different groups (Elkin 1938).

As an introduction to the common, four-section system, one may start with two categories, A and B, and two more categories, 1 and 2. If a person has member ship in both categories, then four status groups result: A1, A2, B1, B2. Assume that there is patrilineal inheritance of A and B; and matrilineal inheritance of 1 and 2 Further assume these groups are exogamous. Therefore, an A1 male must marry a B2 woman. Their children will be A2 because they inherited A membership from father and 2 membership from mother. Following exogamy, these A2 children must marry B1 spouses, thus all four categories are closely linked. A descent system f this type results in *bilinear kin groups* according to Murdock (1949:50–55). Different explanations are provided by Radcliffe-Brown (1931), Levi-Strauss (1949, 1969:146–167), and Romney and Epling (1958). Although the explanations are complex, the structure itself is fairly simple as revealed in a diagram.

EXERCISE 25   Indicate section membership for all the unlabeled symbols n the following diagram.

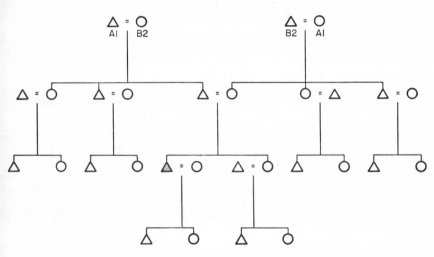

Australians, of course, do not label their groups with letters or numbers. What a particular tribe might understand, for instance, is that a man of the Banaka ection marries a woman of the Burung section; their children belong to Palyeri, who will marry Karimera. Remember that *section membership is not kinship erminology* but you can expect a correspondence between terminology and section nembership. Note how the system puts all parallel cousins in the same section as go while all cross cousins fall into the proper marriageble section. Also notice how ego's sister's children are in a marriageable section in relation to ego's children. As children of siblings of the opposite sex, they are cross cousins to each other. One would expect cross cousin marriage among Australian tribes, and indeed most to practice it. That is, they marry a woman who is in the category of cross cousin f not the actual cross cousin.

Residence Groups

Like marriage, residence is an integral part of kinship, and any analysis of kinship involves close attention to residence patterns. Ecological factors probably re most important in determining where people live and who will reside in a household, but whatever the reasons, residence norms are generally clear cut and have important consequences. Although residence patterns can usually be determined quickly because residence norms are explicit, actual residence may vary considerably from the ideal. Bohannan (1963:87–90) gives examples of difference between residence rules and practices.

Four major patterns of residence recur along with a number of variants Commonly a newly married couple reside with the groom's family of orientation is *patrilocal residence*; if they live instead with the bride's family, the practice i *matrilocal residence*. Generally the residence is better understood as locating with a major grouping, such as a lineage, of one of the spouses. To emphasize this fact Adam (1948) recommends replacing patrilocal with *virilocal* and matrilocal with *uxorilocal*. All four terms will be seen in the literature. Bride and groom may also settle with the groom's MoBr in *avunculocal residence*. In matrilineal societies man inherits a position and power through his MoBr; it makes sense that he resid near the MoBr when he becomes a mature adult through marriage. Finally, th practice familiar to Westerners is *neolocal residence*: The couple is expected t establish a new household.

A number of other alternatives are also well known. Sometimes the coupl may each continue to reside where they did prior to marriage, simply visiting eac other. This *duolocal residence* is feasible in small communities but is uncommor Under a norm termed *bilocal residence*, a couple may also move frequently betwee the bride's and the groom's groupings, in effect maintaining two residences. Finally *matripatrilocal residence* is commonly practiced. Where bride service is required, couple may initially reside with the wife's group for a year or two but move to th husband's group at the end of service. Other varieties of residence are noted b Murdock (1957:670).

It must be emphasized that actual practice generally varies from the norm and fieldworkers should take careful note of practices. Westerners know that neo locality is encouraged and expected but are familiar with cases of married childre residing with parents. College students often know of duolocal residence where marriage is being kept secret.

An analysis of residence appears much simpler than it is; only recentl have anthropologists emphasized the care that must be exercised. Difficulties i such study have been discussed at length by Alland (1963), Barnes (1960) Bohannan (1957), Fischer (1958), and Goodenough (1956a).

Kin Based Groups

The two types of descent, *unilineal* and *bilateral*, lead to two major types o kin groupings. Although Leach (1961) criticizes this division, the typology re mains basic to most analysis of social structure. Bilateral types of organization ar not understood as well as unilineal types even though most anthropologists ar themselves members of bilateral kinship groups. Pehrson (1954) completed on of the first studies; others include Ayoub (1966), Befu (1963), Blehr (1963) Koentjaraningrat (1968), Leyton (1965), Murdock (1964), and Solien (1959)

Bilateral descent can result in fairly large, nonunilineal descent groups Davenport (1959), Ember (1959), Goodenough (1962), Scheffler (1962, 1965) and Firth (1963) analyze examples in depth. Bilateral descent yields an organi ation based on the *kindred*. Essentially the kindred is composed of those relatives recognized by Westerners as "close." Parents, siblings, uncles, aunts, cousins, and their reciprocals—children, nephews, nieces—comprise the kindred. A primary characteristic of the kindred is that the group can only be *temporary* because its membership is focused on a *set of siblings* or an only child. That is, only ego and his siblings are related in an identical way to their cousins. Their MoBrSo and FaSiSo may not consider themselves related. Moreover, at marriage even the siblings no longer share a common kindred. As a result, societies with only bilateral descent can be seen as organized on a basis of overlapping kindreds which shift membership each generation. Because of their temporary nature kindreds usually lack important economic, political, or religious functions. The kindred is visible primarily in times of life crises when it supports ego. It is, of course, particularly important in the entire enculturation process but at a covert level. Freeman (1961: 202–211) and Fox (1965) provide further analysis of the kindred.

Anthropologists have shown much more interest in unilineal descent and the resulting *lineages*. Technically a lineage consists of two or more generations of people consanguineously related through one of the sexes. A man and his children or a woman and her children form a lineage. Only rarely is such a group an operational unit, that is, one that carries out specific tasks. Technically it may be called the *minimal lineage*. In most cases a group that operates from day to day is organized around three or four generations or several siblings of the same sex. This operational group is called a *minor segment* of a lineage. Often minor segments combine for ritual or other events; usually these are segments in the same vicinity. Operating as a larger group, they are termed a *major segment*. Finally, major segments may be combined under the principle that, so long as individuals can trace descent from a common ancestor, they have an important tie; this group is the *maximal lineage*. Possibly such a group may function importantly in warfare; it may also exert some control over marriage. Usually it is more like a category of people than an actual group. Of course the depth of lineages, their size, and functions vary greatly among societies (Barnes, 1962). The fourfold division described above was found useful by Fortes (1940) for a description of Tallensi political organization, but other anthropologists have found no need to break lineages into parts.

Lineages may be characterized by a number of structural features. Fortes' (1953) enumeration of these features brought out the similarity between patrilineages and matrilineages as well as among lineages from different societies. For instance, lineages tend toward being equivalent within a society regardless of their size. Structurally a lineage of twenty members may be equated with one of 300 members. Each lineage operates as a corporate unit; its individual members have legal or political status because of their status within the lineage. Therefore, lineages are generally basic to political organization in many communities.

Recall that another lineage characteristic is *perpetuity*. Unlike the kindred, a lineage continues as long as any member survives; even fictional kin sometimes perpetuate the lineage. As a stable group, lineages can assume rights to land use and ritual as well as political office. Thus, the lineage is associated with primary societal functions that must be denied to the short-lived kindred.

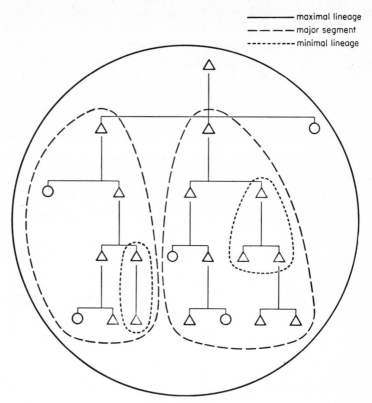

Figure U. Different parts of the lineage.

The importance of the lineage through time is frequently emphasized by the ritual practice of *ancestor veneration*. Since most of a man's statuses and other rights are determined by who his ancestors were, it follows that a man will respect or venerate his lineage founders (Fortes 1961). In some societies the ancestors become godlike and worshipped, but in most cases of "ancestor worship" it may be better understood as veneration through lineage organization.

Fortes' understanding of the common qualities of lineages was a needed improvement over earlier anthropologists who saw great differences between matriliny and patriliny. Much useless debate occurred over which came first. Some important differences recently have been found between the two systems, however. The differences and their implications have been analyzed by a number of anthropologists in a work edited by Schneider and Gough (1961). Their differences are primarily on a psychological rather than sociological order.

The work by Fortes yielded insight into the sociological features that order relationships within descent groups. These features emphasize the stability of lineage organization, and concentration on them makes lineages appear static. The focus overlooks the roles individuals play within the group or the concept that lineage organization might be viewed as process in addition to structure. American anthropologists, such as Roger Keesing (1970), have been analyzing descent groups in Oceania in such a way as to emphasize individual decision making, processual patterns, and the dynamics of lineage organization.

The Clan

The clan is obviously based on kinship because it is a grouping of two or more lineages. Yet, the ties of kinship cannot be traced explicitly; a relationship is assumed. Members of a clan can only "claim" a common mythological ancestor or otherwise account for a common descent.

Because the feelings of closeness within the clan parallel the feelings within a lineage, the clan is almost always exogamous. Structurally norms for exogamy are important in order to emphasize the unilineality of the clan. If a person married within a clan, his children could not make sharp distinctions between paternal and maternal relatives, distinctions emphasized by clan organization. Lowie (1948:237) illustrates the point.

> A Crow in such circumstances loses his bearings and perplexes his tribesmen. For he owes specific obligations to his father's relatives and others to his mother's, who are now hopelessly confounded. The sons of his father's clan ought to be censors; but now the very same persons are his joking relatives and his clan. The dilemma affects others as well as himself.

A final note on the clan involves simple word use. The word "sib" is sometimes used in the way "clan" has been defined here. British social anthropologists regularly use clan for a group of two or more lineages. Some Americans use sib in order to reserve *clan* for a *coresident group* consisting of lineage mates and their spouses. In this usage, a clan for a matrilineal people usually consists of the female descendents of an ancestress, their unmarried brothers, and their husbands. The clan is a face-to-face group that must solve the common recurrent problems of life. The sib must be scattered because of exogamous rules. Whether one uses "clan" or "sib" is unimportant, but it is essential to recognize the difference between the descent grouping and the residence grouping. Most authors will specify how they are using the words.

In summary, students should realize that the analysis of lineages and clans has been basic to social anthropology. Whether these phenomena are the central part of a study (Radcliffe-Brown and Forde 1950) or an indirect, but essential base (Fortes and Evans-Pritchard 1940), social anthropologists in the past have seen lineages and clans as keys to overall social organization. Earlier studies recognized these keys as stable elements. Today many anthropologists (Goodenough, 1970:39–67) are directing their attention to processes within kin groups and the various forms these kin groups may assume. Other anthropologists are concentrating on the change of particular lineal organizations as the descent system becomes bilateral. Although the process must be very widespread, only a few current studies are available (Cohen 1969) and (Spooner 1969). No doubt changing unilineal systems will become as important a topic as the stable, ideal type once was.

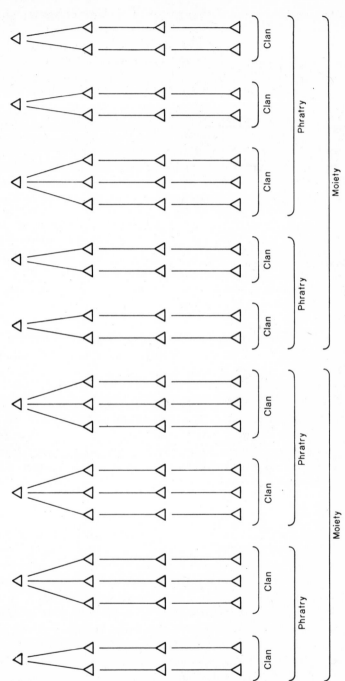

Figure V. Illustration of the possible building blocks of a society.

Phratry and Moiety

Phratry and moiety organization are based on kin ties but are often such rge groups that their link to kinship is nebulous. Lowie (1948:240) describes the ratry as "evidently nothing but a convenient term for a kin linkage." It must be derstood that the linkage involves clans and the phratry is defined as the grouping two or more clans *provided* that *three or more* such groupings of clans occur ithin a society. Where only two major groupings result from a combination of ans, the two groups are termed *moieties* (from French *moitié* meaning half).

The distinction between moiety and phratry is not merely pedantic. A ciety with a dual organization, such as moieties, has many distinctive features at are lacking in societies with three or more major parts. For instance, a balanced nd of opposition between halves brings fairly stable relations (as in a two-party olitical system) between moieties.

In summary, the lineage, clan, phratry, and moiety are forms of organization r linking greater and greater numbers of people through kinship principles as own in Figure V. The clan is a combination of lineages, the phratry a combina- on of clans, and the moiety a combination of clans and/or phratries. The forms organization may be diagrammed as in Figure W to indicate a resemblance th the bureaucracy of modern industry or university. Although only a few tivities clearly follow through a kinship hierarchy the same way they do in a reaucracy, the analogy should indicate that kinship based societies still have number of similarities with urban, industrial, largely non-kin society.

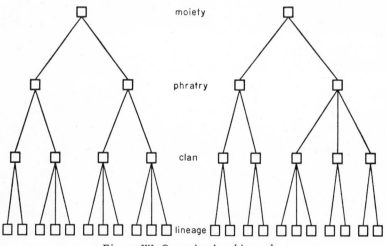

Figure W. Organization hierarchy.

General Review

This second part has introduced more complex forms of social organizatic and a larger number of definitions. For review, the student should not only be ab to define the terms but also see relationships among the grouping.

1. Genealogical method

   Hypothetical kinship schedule

2. Polygyny

   Polyandry

   Serial monogamy

3. Bride wealth

   Bride service

   Sister exchange

4. Parallel cousin marriage

Cross cousin marriage

Unilateral cross cousin marriage

5. Virilocal

Uxorilocal

Avunculocal

Duolocal

Bilocal

6. Corporate group

Lineage

Sib

Clan

Phratry

Moiety

Answers to Exercises

EXERCISE 1 Answer appears on page 9.

EXERCISE 2

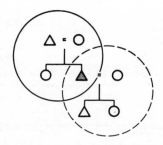

EXERCISE 3

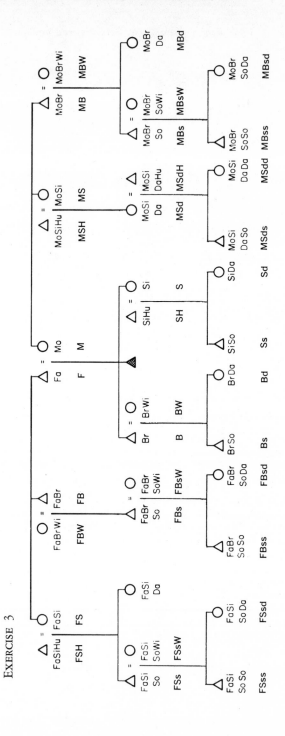

EXERCISE 4   No single answer can be provided. See page 13 for explanation of exercise.

EXERCISE 5

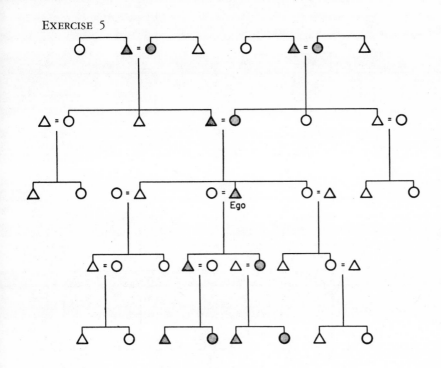

EXERCISE 6

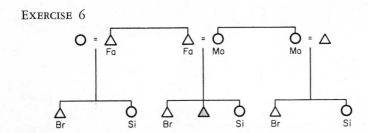

EXERCISE 7

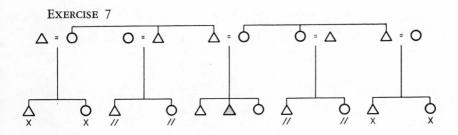

EXERCISE 8

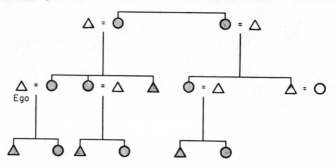

EXERCISE 9

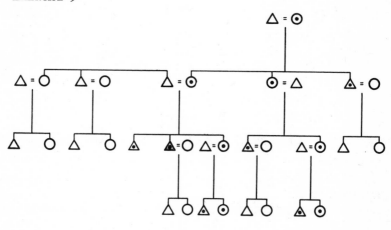

EXERCISE 10

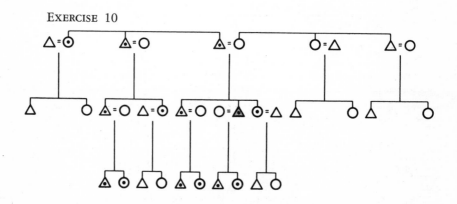

EXERCISE 11

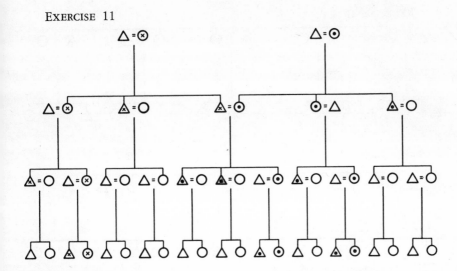

EXERCISE 12

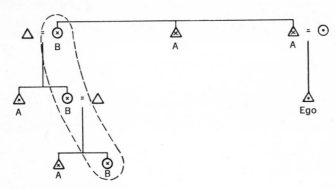

EXERCISE 13   Answer appears on page 33.

EXERCISE 14

1 = E (or Br) because he is the son of an A (or Fa). Remember the rule of uniform descent: If anyone whom ego refers to as A (father) has children whom ego refers to as E (brother), then the children of every A are E.

2 = G (or So) because he is the son of an E. Read the descent rule again, substituting E (Br) for A (Fa) and G (So) for E (Br).

3 = J (or nephew) because he is the son of an F. Uniform descent again explains the term.

4 = G (or So) for the same reason that 2 = G.

5 = H (or Da) a female sibling of a So = Da.

6 = J (or nephew) for the same reason that 3 = J.

EXERCISE 15

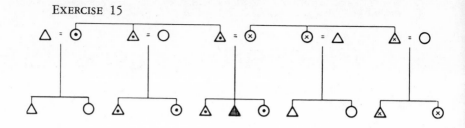

EXERCISE 16

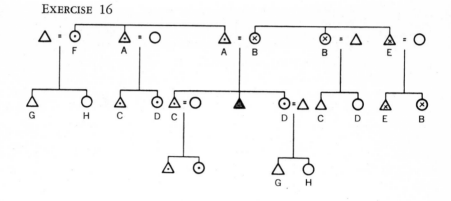

EXERCISE 17

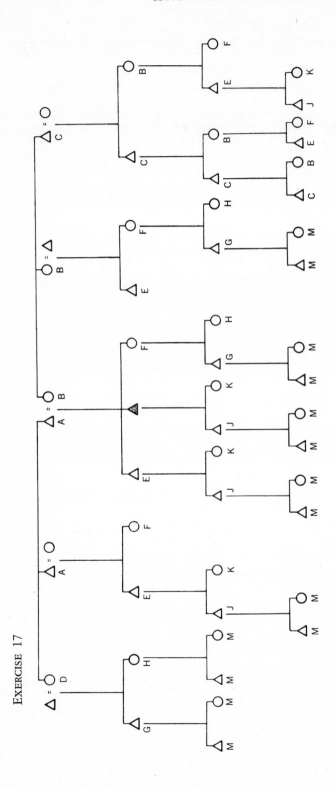

EXERCISE 18   1a Omaha
                1b Bifurcate merging

EXERCISE 19   2a Iroquois
                2b Bifurcate merging

EXERCISE 20   3a Hawaiian
                3b Generational

EXERCISE 21   4a Crow (The North American Indian Tribe of the figur
                     for this exercise is the Crow tribe.)
                4b Bifurcate merging

EXERCISE 22

Grandmother = FaMo
               MoMo

EXERCISE 23   Probably your diagram looked like this one.

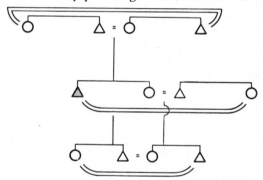

The same diagram, simplified, better illustrates the connection betweer sister exchange and cross-cousin marriage.

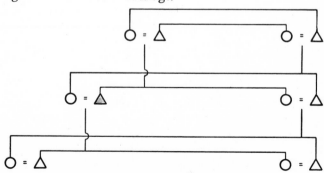

EXERCISE 24

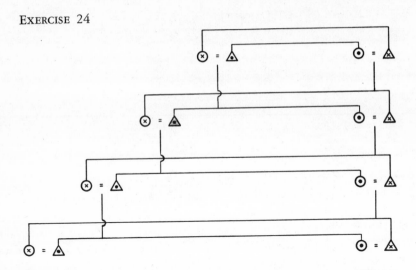

EXERCISE 25

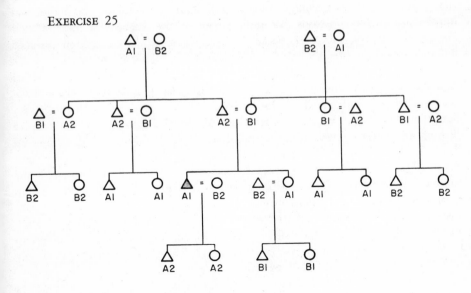

Glossary

THIS GLOSSARY OF KINSHIP TERMS has been added to the workbook for several reasons. First, the student may use it while solving problems in the book. A term not fully defined in the text may be further defined in this glossary. Second, the glossary is intended as a dictionary for future use with other sources of material on kinship. Many articles in professional journals assume readers have a wide knowledge of kinship vocabulary. Where this is not the case, a dictionary of kinship terms is most useful.

In addition to serving as a dictionary, one purpose of the glossary is to clarify some terms with different usages. In building this glossary the author was impressed with the consensus that anthropologists have reached for most of their kinship vocabulary. However, because several basic words have been assigned different meanings, literature on kinship is sometimes difficult to follow.

For instance, a "classificatory term" may be defined as a kinship label applied to numerous sets of different relatives. "Aunt" is a classificatory term which classifies together the mother's sister and the father's sister. On the other hand, "classificatory terminology," as defined by L. H. Morgan, is a system which fails to distinguish between lineal and collateral relatives. In this sense the English word "aunt" is part of a descriptive rather than a classificatory system. However, the most famous—or perhaps infamous—word is "clan." Clan has been defined as 1) any unilineal descent group, 2) a matrilineal descent group, and 3) a residential group consisting of the consanguineal members of one sex, their spouses, and their unmarried siblings. To add to the confusion, the word "gens" has been used for a patrilineal descent group, and "sib" is often used for any unilineal descent group although the Anglo-Saxon sib was never a lineage. The glossary attempts to supply all the meanings for commonly used terms.

In order to prevent adding to the confusion already present, the author has attempted no definitions of his own. To compile the glossary the work of several leading authorities on kinship was analyzed. Murdock (1949) supplies much of the material because his work required explicit definition of kinship vocabulary. In addition writings of Robert Lowie and A. R. Radcliffe-Brown were analyzed; their definitions have been added when they differed from Murdock's or when they aided in clarification. Also works of Fred Eggan, Raymond Firth, Ralph Linton, and Ward Goodenough have been used in the compilation.

A final aim of the glossary is to point up the need for standardizing the few terms with ambiguous or various definitions. Although the meanings of many terms have already been standardized, completion of the task would simplify the teaching of kinship. Consensus also might reduce controversy in kinship theory because some disagreement is a matter of semantics rather than analysis. Possibly agreement might even reduce the vocabulary. Leach (1962:131) has made plain the need for simplification: "We now have unilineal descent, non-unilineal descent, bilateral descent, double descent and even pseudo-double descent (whatever that means). I must protest most strongly. This is not the language of science but of gobbledygook."

ADDRESS, TERM OF: A kinship term used when speaking to or addressing a relative. *See* Reference, Term of; Teknonymy.

ADELPHIC POLANDRY: The marriage of a woman to two or more brothers; also called fraternal polyandry.

AFFINAL RELATIVES: Those relatives connected by one or more marital links. *See* Consanguineal.

AGAMY: The lack of any rule in regard to marriage within or without of a group; it denotes absence of marriage regulations on the part of a social unit.

AGNATES: Male or female descendants by male links from the same male ancestor.

AMITACLAN: A clan with patrilineal descent in which unmarried females reside with a paternal aunt and bring their husbands to the FaSi home; it parallels the avuncuclan, but is only theoretical.

AMITALOCAL RESIDENCE: A theoretical norm whereby wives take their husbands to the residence of the bride's father's sister; it parallels avunculocal residence, but no case has been found.

ASYMMETRICAL CROSS COUSIN MARRIAGE: An institution allowing a male ego to marry only the MoBrDa (matrilateral asymmetry) or only the FaSiDa (patrilateral asymmetry).

AVOIDANCE RELATIONSHIP: A pattern of complete avoidance of speech and physical contact between relatives. Murdock (1949:273) suggests that such a technique is an aspect of sex regulation in societies where sexual prohibitions are not strongly internalized in enculturation; in the same place he briefly summarizes theories of Eggan and Radcliffe-Brown.

AVUNCUCLAN: A matrisib localized around male rather than female members. It is formed through avunculocal residence; that is, males leave their home to live with MoBr and continue to reside there after marriage.

AVUNCULOCAL RESIDENCE: A norm in which unmarried males leave their paternal homes to reside with a MoBr; upon marriage their wives are brought into the household.

BIFURCATE COLLATERAL TERMINOLOGY: A system which differentiates the uncles and aunts both from parents and from each other.

BIFURCATE MERGING TERMINOLOGY: A system which groups the Fa and FaBr, and the Mo and MoSi; however, the MoBr and FaSi are denoted by distinct terms.

BILATERAL DESCENT: A practice which links a person with a group of close relatives through both sexes; it limits the number of close relatives by excluding some of both the father's kin group and the mother's kin group.

BILINEAR KIN GROUP: Persons affiliated with one another by both patrilineal and matrilineal ties, including those who stand to one another in such relationships as own siblings, parallel cousins, paternal grandfather and son's child, and maternal grandmother and daughter's child (Murdock 1949:51).

BILOCAL RESIDENCE: A norm which permits a married couple to live with or near the parents of either spouse; a factor such as relative wealth of the two families is likely to determine where the couple will reside.

BRIDE PRICE: Compensation to parents for the loss of a daughter who leaves her home when she marries; it is commonly a guarantee that the wife will be well treated in her new home. Also termed bride wealth or progeny wealth.

CLAN: A compromise kin group based on a rule of residence and a rule of descent. A unilocal rule of residence combines with a unilinear rule of descent. Some affinal relatives are included and some consanguineal kinsmen excluded (Murdock 1949:66). The clan is a grouping composed of a number of lineages (Firth 1951:53).

CLAN-BARRIO: A clan that resides in a ward of a village or in a hamlet of a community. The community is composed of clan-barrios.

CLASSIFICATORY TERMINOLOGY: Kinship terms which do not distinguish between lineal and collateral relatives. The Hawaiian type of kinship, which ignores differences between father and uncle or brother and cousin, is classificatory. *See* Descriptive Terminology.

COGNATIC KIN: Relatives by genealogical ties without particular emphasis on either patrilineal or matrilineal connections; also has been described as nonunilineal descent. Formerly defined as those related on the mother's side, in contrast with agnatic kin; such kin are now known as "uterine."

COMPOUND FAMILY: A unit consisting of three or more spouses and their children; it may be produced in monogamous societies by a second marriage giving rise to step-relationships. *See* Extended Family.

CONSANGUINEAL: Relatives whose every connecting link is one of "blood" or common ancestry.

CORESIDENCE: Local or territorial contiguity. Anthropologists once separated a principle of kinship from one of coresidence by claiming an evolution from the former to the latter; however, ties of coresidence mingle with kinship in establishing solidarity.

CROSS COUSIN: The child of a father's sister or of a mother's brother; the children of siblings of opposite sex are cross cousins.

DEME (pronounced "deem"): A local group lacking unilineal descent.

DERIVATIVE KINSHIP TERM: A term that is a compound of an elementary kin term and another sound or phrase, for example, "sister-in-law" or "stepson."

DESCENT: A rule of descent affiliates an individual at birth with a group of relatives; this intimate group provides extensive rights and obligations. Descent can be patrilineal, matrilineal, or bilateral.

DESCRIPTIVE KINSHIP TERM: A term that combines two or more elementary terms to denote a specific relative. "My brother's wife" is a descriptive term while "sister-in-law" is not. A sister-in-law may be either a WiSi or BrWi. (One must be careful to distinguish between descriptive terminology or systems on the one hand and descriptive terms on the other. Descriptive systems separate lineal from collateral relatives. Thus, "cousin" is a term in a descriptive system. However, the term "cousin" may be called a classificatory term because it includes several different types of relatives.)

DESCRIPTIVE TERMINOLOGY: Kinship terms which set off the direct line of a person's descent and the immediate relatives of his own generation from all other individuals. Lineal relatives are all differentiated from collateral relatives.

DOUBLE DESCENT: A practice in which an individual belongs to one group through matrilineal descent, another group through patrilineal descent. Frequently, different types of property are inherited through the different sexes.

DUOLOCAL RESIDENCE: A norm which requires bride and groom to remain in their original locales, thus maintaining two residences.

ELEMENTARY FAMILY: A unit consisting of a man, his wife, and their child or children. A childless couple would not constitute an elementary family. *See* Nuclear Family.

ELEMENTARY KINSHIP TERM: A term that cannot be reduced into component elements. "Father" and "niece" are elementary terms in English.

ENDODEME: An endogamous local group lacking a descent rule.

ENDOGAMY: A rule of marriage that requires a person to take a spouse from within the local, kin, status, or other group to which the person belongs.

EXOGAMY: A rule of marriage that requires a person to marry outside local, kin, status, or other such group to which a person belongs.

EXTENDED FAMILY: A unit composed of two or more nuclear families linked by consanguineal ties. *See* Compound Family.

FAMILY OF ORIENTATION: One in which ego is born and reared; it includes Fa, Mo, and siblings.

FAMILY OF PROCREATION: One that ego forms by marriage; it includes his spouse or spouses and children.

FILIAL WIDOW INHERITANCE: The norm that allows a man to inherit his father's widows as wives, except his own mother. It can occur only in polygynous tribes but even then is rare.

FRATERNAL JOINT FAMILY: A unit composed of two or more brothers and their wives; the bond of union is consanguineal.

GROUP MARRIAGE: A marital union of several men and several women. It probably never occurs as a norm but does appear in exceptional individual instances.

HYPERGAMY: Social class exogamy; a woman is expected to marry into a group superior to her own.

INCEST: Sexual intercourse between two persons who are related by a real, assumed, or artificial bond of kinship that is regarded as a bar to sex relations.

Where sex relations are forbidden, but not because of kinship, their practice is called *mismating.*

Where either party occupies a status forbidding sex relations, e.g., a nun, sexual intercourse may be termed *status unchastity* (Murdock 1949:261).

JOKING RELATIONSHIP: Patterned behavior between relatives that calls for mild to taunting or ribald joking.

KINDRED: A group closely related to ego through both sexes; it furnishes him with certain rights and obligations. Because of the structure of bilaterality, a kindred is never the same for any two persons except siblings.

KIN GROUPS: Any social grouping based on kinship ties.

LEVIRATE: A custom whereby a widow preferably marries a brother of her deceased husband.

LINEAGE: A consanguineal kin group practicing unilineal descent, which includes only persons who can actually trace their relationship to a common ancestor; that is, a lineage is all the unilineal descendants of a known common ancestor or ancestress.

MATRIARCHATE: Rule of the family by the mother; no strictly matriarchal peoples are known. *Matripotestal* is a synonym for matriarchal.

MATRICLAN: A residence group of females, the unmarried males of the women's clans, and the husbands and the children of the married females.

MATRILINEAL DESCENT: A system which associates ego with kin consisting exclusively of relatives through females.

MATRILOCAL RESIDENCE: A norm which requires the groom to leave his paternal home and live with his bride, either nearby or in the house of her parents.

MATRIPATRILOCAL RESIDENCE: A pattern of initial matrilocal residence followed by permanent patrilocal residence.

MERGING: The grouping of lineal and collateral kinsmen under one classificatory term. Classifying the FaBr with Fa or MoSi with Mo is a common merging practice.

MIXED DESCENT: Gillin (1948:433) notes that mixed descent is relatively rare but two varieties do occur. Sex-linked mixed descent affiliates males with their father's male line; females with the mother's female line. Cross-sex mixed descent affiliates males with the mother's line. Cross-sex mixed descent affiliates males with the mother's father, females with the father's mother.

MOIETY: When a society is divided into two groups so that every person is necessarily a member of one or the other, the dichotomy results in so many distinctive features that a special term, moiety, is applied to them (Murdock 1949:47).

NEOLOCAL RESIDENCE: The establishment of an independent household.

NEPOTIC INHERITANCE: The norm that a man inherits his uncle's wife or wives. It has been found in patrilineal groups but fits more logically a matrilineal framework, where it is usually found. It is far from universal with matrilineal descent, however.

NUCLEAR FAMILY: A unit consisting typically of a married man and woman with their offspring. *See* Elementary Family.

PARALLEL COUSINS: The children of siblings of the same sex. The children of a father's brother and a mother's sister are parallel cousins.

PATRICLAN: A residential group of male clan mates and their wives plus the unmarried females of the clan.

PATRILINEAL DESCENT: A system which affiliates ego with a group of kinsmen, all of whom are related to him through males.

PATRILOCAL RESIDENCE: A norm which requires the bride to reside with the groom either nearby or in the home of the groom's parents.

PHRATRY: A group of two or more sibs that recognizes a purely conventional unilinear bond of kinship (Murdock 1949:47).

The phratry is a group of two or more clans united for certain common objects. They may or may not be exogamous (Lowie 1948:338).

Note that Murdock claims the tie is kinship-based, and that Lowie maintains the bond is one of common interest.

POLYANDRY: The marriage of one woman to two or more men at the same time.

POLYGYNY: The marriage of one man to two or more women at the same time.

PSEUDO-RELATIONS: A socially defined equivalent of affinal or consanguine ties.

RAMAGE: A grouping of two or more lineages. Unlike the sib, however, the descent of the lineages is *ambilineal* or *nonunilineal*. Descent may be traced through either a male or a female. Firth (1936) uses the term to emphasize the process of fission rather than exogamy. Ramage organization is common in Polynesia and occurs elsewhere in the world.

Murdock (1960:11) defines ramages as the functional equivalent of lineages, but unlike lineages, ego has some choice of membership reckoning descent through either males or females. Like lineages, the ramage group is consanguineal and susceptible to segmentation.

REFERENCE, TERM OF: One used in speaking about a relative. One speaks of a nephew but rarely addresses him as "Nephew." *See* Address.

RESPECT RELATIONSHIPS: Behavior patterns between kin that involves standardized ways of showing respect.

SIB: Two or more lineages related by a common, mythical ancestor. *See* Clan.

SISTER EXCHANGE: A mode of contracting marriage whereby a sister or other female relative is exchanged for a wife.

SORORAL POLYGYNY: The preferred union of one man with two or more sisters.

SORORATE: A custom whereby a widower preferably marries a sister of his deceased wife.

SYMMETRICAL CROSS COUSIN MARRIAGE: Marriage with either the MoBrDa or FaSiDa. The practice is also described as bilateral cross cousin marriage.

TEKNONYMY: A practice whereby a child does not take its name from its parents but rather parents derive a name from their child. For example, an adult is known as "the father of so-and-so".

ULTIMOGENITURE: A rule which favors the youngest-born child in a family; its contrasts with primogeniture.

UNILINEAL DESCENT: The tracing of relationship through either the male or the female line. *See* Descent.

UTERINE RELATIVES: Those kin related to ego through his mother.

UTERINE NEPHEW: Ego's sister's son.

UXORILOCAL: A synonym for matrilocal but connotes that a couple lives with the wife's lineage rather than with the mother.

VIRILOCAL: A synonym for patrilocal but connotes that a couple lives with the husband's lineage rather than with the father.

Bibliography

ACKERMAN, CHARLES, 1964, "Structure and Statistics: The Purum Case," *American Anthropologist*, 66:53–66.

ADAM, LEONHARD, 1948, " 'Virilocal' and 'Uxorilocal'," *Man*, 48:12.

ALLAND, ALEXANDER, 1963, "Residence, Domicile, and Descent Groups among the Abron of the Ivory Coast," *Ethnology*, 2:276–281.

ALTSCHULER, MILTON, 1965, "Notes on Cayapa Kinship," *Ethnology*, 4:440–447.

AYOUB, MILLICENT, 1966, "The Family Reunion," *Ethnology*, 5:415–433.

BARNES, J. A., 1960, "Marriage and Residential Continuity," *American Anthropologist*, 62:850–866.

———, 1962, "African Models in the New Guinea Highlands," *Man*, 62:5–9.

BARNETT, H. G., 1960, *Being a Palauan.* New York: Holt, Rinehart and Winston.

BASSO, KEITH, 1970, *The Cibecue Apache.* New York: Holt, Rinehart and Winston.

BEATTIE, JOHN, 1960, *Bunyoro, An African Kingdom.* New York: Holt, Rinehart and Winston.

BEFU, HARUMI, 1963, "Patrilineal Descent and Personal Kindred in Japan," *American Anthropologist*, 65:1328–1341.

———, and LEONARD PLOTNICOV, 1962, "Types of Corporate Unilineal Descent Groups," *American Anthropologist*, 64:313–327.

BERTING, J. and H. PHILIPSEN, 1960, "Solidarity, Stratification and Sentiments," *Bijdragen Tot de Taal-Land-en Volkenkunde*, 116:55–80.

BLEHR, OTTO, 1963, "Action Groups in a Society with Bilateral Kinship: A Case Study from the Faroe Islands," *Ethnology*, 2:269–275.

BOHANNAN, PAUL, 1957, "An Alternate Residence Classification," *American Anthropologist*, 59:126–131.

———, 1963, *Social Anthropology.* New York: Holt, Rinehart and Winston.

———, and JOHN MIDDLETON, 1968, *Kinship and Social Organization.* Garden City, N.Y.: Natural History Press.

BRUNER, EDWARD, 1955, "Two Processes of Change in Mandan-Hidatsa Kinship Terminology," *American Anthropologist*, 57:840–850.

BUCHLER, IRA and HENRY SELBY, 1968, *Kinship and Social Organization.* New York: The Macmillan Company.

BURLING, ROBBINS, 1963, "Garo Kinship Terms and the Analysis of Meaning," *Ethnology*, 2:70–85.

———, 1964, "Cognition and Componential Analysis: God's Truth or Hocus-Pocus?," *American Anthropologist*, 66:20–28.

CHAGNON, NAPOLEON, 1968, *Yąnomamö, The Fierce People.* New York: Holt, Rinehart and Winston.

COHEN, MYRON, 1969, "Agnatic Kinship in Taiwan," *Ethnology*, 8:167–182.

CONANT, FRANCIS, 1961, "Jarawa Kin Systems of Reference and Address: A Componential Comparison," *Anthropological Linguistics*, 3:19–33.

COULT, ALLAN, 1962a, "An Analysis of Needham's Critique of the Homans and Schneider Theory," *Southwestern Journal of Anthropology*, 18:317–335.

————, 1962b, "The Determinants of Differential Cross-Cousin Marriage," *Man*, 62:34–36.

DAVENPORT, WILLIAM, 1959, "Nonunilinear Descent and Descent Groups," *American Anthropologist*, 61:557–572.

DOLE, GERTRUDE, 1960, "The Classification of Yankee Nomenclature in the Light of Evolution in Kinship," in *Essays in the Science of Culture*, GERTRUDE DOLE and ROBERT CARNEIRO, eds. New York: Thomas Y. Crowell Co.

————, 1969, "Generation Kinship Nomenclature as an Adaptation to Endogamy," *Southwestern Journal of Anthropology*, 25:105–123.

DOWNS, JAMES, 1966, *The Two Worlds of the Washo*. New York: Holt, Rinehart and Winston.

DOZIER, EDWARD, 1966, *Hano: A Tewa Indian Community in Arizona*. New York: Holt, Rinehart and Winston.

EGGAN, FRED, 1937, "Historical Changes in the Choctaw Kinship System," *American Anthropologist*, 39:34–52.

————, 1950, *Social Organization of the Western Pueblos*. Chicago: University of Chicago Press.

————, 1955, *Social Anthropology of North American Tribes*, enlarged ed. Chicago: University of Chicago Press.

————, 1960, "Lewis H. Morgan in Kinship Perspective," in *Essays in the Science of Culture*, GERTRUDE DOLE and ROBERT CARNEIRO, eds. New York: Thomas Y. Crowell Co.

————, 1966, *The American Indian*. Chicago: Aldine Publishing Co.

————, JACK GOODY and JULIAN PITT-RIVERS, 1968, "Kinship," *International Encyclopedia of the Social Sciences*. New York: The Macmillan Company and The Free Press.

ELKIN, A. P., 1954, *The Australian Aborigines*, 3d ed. Sydney: Angus and Robertson.

EMBER, MELVIN, 1959, "The Nonunilinear Descent Groups in Samoa," *American Anthropologist*, 61:573–577.

EVANS-PRITCHARD, E. E., 1929, "The Study of Kinship in Primitive Societies," *Man*, 29:190–93.

EYDE, DAVID and PAUL POSTAL, 1961, "Avunculocality and Incest: The Development of Unilateral Cross Cousin Marriage and Crow-Omaha Kinship Systems," *American Anthropologist*, 63:747–771.

FARBER, BERNARD, 1968, *Comparative Kinship Systems*. New York: John Wiley & Sons, Inc.

FARON, LOUIS, 1962, "Marriage, Residence, and Domestic Group among the Panamanian Choco," *Ethnology*, 1:13–38.

————, 1968, *The Mapuche Indians of Chile*. New York: Holt, Rinehart and Winston.

FATHAUER, GEORGE, 1961, "Trobriand," in *Matrilineal Kinship*, DAVID SCHNEIDER and KATHLEEN GOUGH, eds. Berkeley: University of California Press.

FIRTH, RAYMOND, 1936, *We, the Tikopia*. London: George Allen & Unwin, Ltd.

————, 1951, *Elements of Social Organization*. London: C. A. Watts & Co., Ltd.

————, 1963, "Bilateral Descent Groups: An Operational Viewpoint," Occasional Paper in *Studies in Kinship and Marriage*, I. SCHAPERA, ed. London: Royal Anthropological Institute.

FISHER, J. L., 1958, "The Classification of Residence in Census," *American Anthropologist*, 60:508–517.

FORTES, MEYER, 1940, "The Political System of the Tallensi of the Northern Territories of the Gold Coast," in *African Political Systems*, MEYER FORTES and A. R. RADCLIFFE-BROWN, eds. London: Oxford University Press.

————, 1953, "The Structure of Unilineal Descent Groups," *American Anthropologist*, 55:17–41.

———, 1959, "Descent, Filiation and Affinity," *Man,* 59:193–197, 206–212.

———, 1961, "Pietas in Ancestor Worship," *Journal of the Royal Anthropological Institute,* 91:166–191.

———, 1969, *Kinship and the Social Order: The Legacy of Lewis Henry Morgan.* Chicago: Aldine Publishing Co.

———, and E. E. EVANS-PRITCHARD, eds., 1940, *African Political Systems.* London: Oxford University Press.

FOX, ROBIN, 1965, "Prolegomena to the Study of British Kinship," in *Penguin Survey of the Social Sciences,* JULIUS GOULD, ed. Baltimore: Penguin Books.

———, 1967, *Kinship and Marriage.* Baltimore: Penguin Books.

FREEDMAN, MAURICE, 1965, "Systems of Descent," *Encyclopaedia Britannica.* Chicago: William Benton Publishers.

FREEMAN, J. D., 1961, "On the Concept of the Kindred," *Journal of the Royal Anthropological Institute,* 91:192–220.

GALLIN, BERNARD, 1963, "Cousin-Marriage in China," *Ethnology,* 2:104–108.

GIBBS, JAMES, 1964, "Social Organization," in *Horizons of Anthropology,* SOL TAX, ed. Chicago: Aldine Publishing Co.

GILLIN, JOHN, 1948, *The Ways of Men.* New York: Appleton-Century-Crofts.

GOLDSCHMIDT, WALTER, 1960, *Exploring the Ways of Mankind.* New York: Holt, Rinehart and Winston.

GOODENOUGH, WARD, 1951, *Property, Kin and Community on Truk.* Yale University Publication in Anthropology, No. 46. New Haven, Conn.: Yale University Press.

———, 1956a, "Residence Rules," *Southwestern Journal of Anthropology,* 12:22–37.

———, 1956b, "Componential Analysis and the Study of Meaning," *Language,* 32:195–216.

———, 1962, "Kindred and Hamlet in Lakalai, New Britain," *Ethnology,* 1:5–12.

———, 1965, "Yankee Kinship Terminology: A Problem in Componential Analysis," *American Anthropologist,* 67 (5):259–287 (special edition).

———, 1970, *Description and Comparison in Cultural Anthropology.* Chicago: Aldine Publishing Co.

GOODY, JACK, 1959, "The Mother's Brother and the Sister's Son in West Africa," *Journal of the Royal Anthropological Institute,* 89:61–88.

GOUGH, KATHLEEN, 1961, "Nayar," in *Matrilineal Kinship,* DAVID SCHNEIDER and KATHLEEN GOUGH, eds. Berkeley: University of California Press.

HOCART, ARTHUR, 1937, "Kinship Systems," *Anthropos,* 32:545–551.

HOMANS, GEORGE and DAVID SCHNEIDER, 1955, *Marriage, Authority, and Final Cause.* New York: The Free Press of Glencoe.

HOPKINS, NICHOLAS, 1969, "A Formal Account of Chalchihuitan Tzotzil Kinship Terminology." *Ethnology,* 8:85–102.

HSU, FRANCIS, 1965, "The Effect of Dominant Kinship Relationships on Kin and Non-Kin Behavior: A Hypothesis," *American Anthropologist,* 67:638–661.

———, ed., 1970, *Kinship and Culture.* Chicago: Aldine Publishing Co.

HUNT, EVA, 1969, "The Meaning of Kinship in San Juan: Genealogical and Sociological Models," *Ethnology,* 8:37–53.

JOSSELIN DE JONG, JAN P., 1952, *Levi-Strauss' Theory on Kinship and Marriage,* Mededlingen van het Rijkmuseum voor Volkenkunde, No. 10, Leiden: Brill.

KEESING, FELIX, 1958, *Cultural Anthropology,* New York: Holt, Rinehart and Winston.

KEESING, ROGER, 1970, "Shrines, Ancestors, and Cognatic Descent: The Kwaio and Tallensi," *American Anthropologist,* 72:755–775.

KOENTJARANINGRAT, 1968, "Javanese Data on the Unresolved Problems of the Kindred," *Ethnology,* 7:53–58.

KOTTAK, CONRAD, 1967, "Kinship and Class in Brazil," *Ethnology,* 6:427–444.

KROEBER, ALFRED, 1909, "Classificatory Systems of Relationship," *Journal of the Royal Anthropological Institute,* 39:77–84.

LANDAR, HERBERT, 1962, "Fluctuation of Forms in Navaho Kinship Terminology," *American Anthropologist,* 64:985–1000.

LANE, ROBERT, 1962, "Patrilateral Cross-Cousin Marriage: Structural Analysis and Ethnographic Cases," *Ethnology,* 1:467–499.

————, and BARBARA LANE, 1959, "On the Development of Dakota-Iroquois and Crow-Omaha Kinship Terminologies," *Southwestern Journal of Anthropology,* 15:254–265.

LANGE, CHARLES, 1959, *Cochiti: A New Mexico Pueblo, Past and Present.* Austin: University of Texas Press.

————, 1967, "Historical Reconstruction: Problems in Cochiti Culture History," in *American Historical Anthropology,* CARROLL RILEY and WALTER TAYLOR, eds. Carbondale and Edwardsville: Southern Illinois University Press.

LEACH, EDMOND, 1957, "Aspects of Bridewealth and Marriage Stability Among the Kachin and Lakher," *Man,* 57:50–55.

————, 1961, *Rethinking Anthropology.* London: The Athlone Press.

————, 1962, "On Certain Unconsidered Aspects of Double Descent Systems," *Man,* 63:130–34.

LESSA, WILLIAM, 1966, *Ulithi: A Micronesian Design for Living.* New York: Holt, Rinehart and Winston.

LEVI-STRAUSS, CLAUDE, 1962, *Totemism.* Boston: The Beacon Press.

————, 1963, *Structural Anthropology.* New York: Basic Books, Inc.

————, 1969, *The Elementary Structures of Kinship.* Boston: The Beacon Press. Published in France in 1949 as *Les Structures elementaires de la Parente.*

LEYTON, ELLIOTT, 1965, "Composite Descent Groups in Canada," *Man,* 65:107–10.

LINTON, RALPH, 1924, "Totemism and the A.E.F.," *American Anthropologist,* 26:296–300.

————, 1936, *The Study of Man.* New York: Appleton-Century-Crofts.

LIVINGSTONE, FRANK, 1959, "A Formal Analysis of Prescriptive Marriage Systems among the Australian Aborigines," *Southwestern Journal of Anthropology,* 15:361–72.

LOUNSBURY, FLOYD, 1956, "A Semantic Analysis of the Pawnee Kinship Usage," *Language,* 32:158–194.

————, 1964, "The Formal Analysis of Crow- and Omaha-Type Kinship Terminologies," in *Explorations in Cultural Anthropology,* WARD GOODENOUGH, ed. New York: McGraw-Hill, Inc.

LOWIE, ROBERT, 1935, *The Crow Indians.* New York: Holt, Rinehart and Winston.

————, 1948, *Social Organization.* New York: Holt, Rinehart and Winston.

————, and FRED EGGAN, 1965, "Kinship Terminology," *Encyclopaedia Britannica.* Chicago: William Benton Publishers.

MALINOWSKI, BRONISLAW, 1927, *Sex and Repression in Savage Society.* London: Routledge & Kegan Paul Ltd.

————, 1929, *The Sexual Life of Savages.* London: Routledge & Kegan Paul Ltd.

————, 1960, "A Woman-Centered Family System," in *Exploring the Ways of Mankind,* WALTER GOLDSCHMIDT, ed. New York: Holt, Rinehart and Winston.

MATTHEWS, G. H., 1959, "Proto-Siouan Kinship Terminology," *American Anthropologist,* 61:252–278.

MIDDLETON, JOHN, 1965, *The Lugbara of Uganda.* New York: Holt, Rinehart and Winston.

MINTZ, SIDNEY and ERIC WOLF, 1950, "An Analysis of Ritual Co-Parenthood (Compadrazgo)," *Southwestern Journal of Anthropology,* 6:341–368.

MOORE, SALLY, 1963, "Oblique and Asymmetrical Cross-Cousin Marriage and Crow-Omaha Terminology," *American Anthropologist,* 65:296–311.

MORGAN, LEWIS HENRY, 1870, *Systems of Consanguinity and Affinity,* Smithsonian Institution Contributions to Knowledge, Vol. 17, No. 218. Washington: Smithsonian Institution.

————, 1877, *Ancient Society.* New York: Henry Holt and Company.

MURDOCK, GEORGE, 1949, *Social Structure.* New York: The Macmillan Company.

————, 1957, "World Ethnographic Sample," *American Anthropologist,* 59:664–687.

————, 1960, "Cognatic Forms of Social Organization," in *Social Structure in Southeast Asia,* GEORGE MURDOCK, ed. Chicago: Quadrangle Books.

————, 1964, "The Kindred," *American Anthropologist,* 66:129–132.

MURPHY, ROBERT, and LEONARD KASDAN, 1959, "The Structure of Parallel Cousin Marriage," *American Anthropologist,* 61:17–29.

NEEDHAM, RODNEY, 1958, "The Formal Analysis of Prescriptive Patrilateral Cross-Cousin Marriage," *Southwestern Journal of Anthropology,* 14:199–219.

————, 1960, "Patrilateral Prescriptive Alliance and the Ungarinyin," *Southwestern Journal of Anthropology,* 16:274–291.

————, 1961, "Analytical Note on the Structure of Siriono Society," *Southwestern Journal of Anthropology,* 17:239–255.

————, 1962a, *Structure and Sentiment.* Chicago: University of Chicago Press.

————, 1962b, "Genealogy and Category in Wikmunkan Society," *Ethnology* 1:223–264.

OPLER, MORRIS, 1947, "Rule and Practice in the Behavioral Pattern Between Jicarilla Apache Affinal Relatives," *American Anthropologist,* 49:453–462.

PEHRSON, ROBERT, 1954, "The Lappish Herding Leader: A Structural Analysis," *American Anthropologist,* 56:1076–1080.

POSPISIL, LEOPOLD, 1964, *The Kapauku Papuans.* New York: Holt, Rinehart and Winston.

————, and WILLIAM LAUGHLIN, 1963, "Kinship Terminology and Kindred among the Nunamiut Eskimo," *Ethnology,* 2:180–189.

RADCLIFFE-BROWN, A. R., 1924, "The Mother's Brother in South Africa," *South Africa Journal of Science,* 21:542–555.

————, 1931, "The Social Organization of Australian Tribes," *Oceania Monograph* No. 1.

————, 1952, *Structure and Function in Primitive Society.* New York: The Free Press of Glencoe.

————, and DARYLL FORDE, eds., 1950, *African Systems of Kinship and Marriage.* London: Oxford University Press.

RILEY, CARROLL and WALTER TAYLOR, eds., 1967, *American Historical Anthropology.* Carbondale and Edwardsville: Southern Illinois University Press.

RIVERS, W. H. R., 1910, "The Genealogical Method of Anthropological Inquiry," *The Sociological Review,* 3:1–12. Reprinted 1968 in *Kinship and Social Organization,* Monographs on Social Organization. London: London School of Economics.

————, 1914, *Kinship and Social Organization.* London: Oxford University Press.

ROMNEY, A. KIMBALL, 1965, "Kalmuk Mongol and the Classification of Lineal Kinship Terminologies," *American Anthropologist,* 67(5)127–141 (special edition).

————, and PHILIP EPLING, 1958, "A Simplified Model of Kariera Kinship," *American Anthropologist,* 60:59–74:

SAHLINS, MARSHALL, 1961, "The Segmentary Lineage: An Organization of Predatory Expansion," *American Anthropologist,* 63:322–345.

SCHEFFLER, HAROLD, 1962, "Kindred and Kin Groups in Simbo Island Social Structure," *Ethnology,* 1:135–157.

————, 1965, *Choiseul Island Social Structure.* Berkeley: University of California Press.

SCHNEIDER, DAVID, 1963, "Some Muddles in the Models; or How the System Really

Works," in *The Relevance of Models for Social Anthropology,* M. BANTON, ed. Monograph No. 1. Association of Social Anthropologists.

———, 1965, "American Kin Terms for Kinsmen: A Critique of Goodenough's Componential Analysis of Yankee Kinship Terminology." *American Anthropologist,* 67(5)288–308 (special edition).

———, 1968, *American Kinship: A Cultural Account.* Englewood Cliffs: Prentice-Hall, Inc.

———, and GEORGE HOMANS, 1955, "Kinship Terminology and the American Kinship System," *American Anthropologist,* 57:1194–1208.

———, and KATHLEEN GOUGH, eds., 1961, *Matrilineal Kinship.* Berkeley: University of California Press.

SELBY, HENRY, 1970, "Continuities and Prospects in Anthropological Studies," *Current Directions in Anthropology.* Bulletin of the American Anthropological Association, 3(3):2.

SERVICE, ELMAN, 1962, *Primitive Social Organization.* New York: Random House, Inc.

SOLIEN, NANCIE, 1959, "The Nonunilinear Descent Group in the Caribbean and Central America," *American Anthropologist,* 61:578–583.

SPIER, LESLIE, 1925, "The Distribution of Kinship Systems in North America," *University of Washington, Publications in Anthropology,* 1:69–88.

SPIRO, MELFORD, 1964, "Causes, Functions and Cross-Cousin Marriage: An Essay in Anthropological Explanation," *Journal of the Royal Anthropological Institute,* 94:30–43.

SPOEHR, ALEXANDER, 1947, "Changing Kinship Systems," *Field Museum of Natural History, Anthropological Series,* 33:153–325.

SPOONER, BRIAN, 1969, "Politics, Kinship, and Ecology in Southeast Persia," *Ethnology,* 8:139–152.

TAX, SOL, 1955a, "Some Problems of Social Organization," in *Social Anthropology of North American Tribes,* FRED EGGAN, ed., enlarged ed. Chicago: University of Chicago Press.

———, 1955b, "From Lafitau to Radcliffe-Brown," in *Social Anthropology of North American Tribes,* FRED EGGAN, ed., enlarged ed. Chicago: University of Chicago Press.

TRIGGER, BRUCE, 1969, *The Huron: Farmers of the North.* New York: Holt, Rinehart and Winston.

TURNER, VICTOR, 1969, *The Ritual Process: Structure and Anti-Structure.* Chicago: Aldine Publishing Co.

TYLOR, EDWARD, 1889, "On a Method of Investigating the Development of Institutions; Applied to the Laws of Marriage and Descent," *Journal of the Royal Anthropological Institute,* 18:245–272.

UCHENDU, VICTOR, 1965, *The Igbo of Southeast Nigeria.* New York: Holt, Rinehart and Winston.

VAN GENNEP, ARNOLD, 1960, *The Rites of Passage.* Chicago: University of Chicago Press. Published in France in 1908 as *Les Rites de Passage.*

VOGET, FRED, 1953, "Kinship Changes at Caughnawaga," *American Anthropologist,* 55:385–394.

WALLACE, ANTHONY, 1962, "Culture and Cognition," *Science,* 135:351–357.

———, and JOHN ATKINS, 1960, "The Meaning of Kinship Terms," *American Anthropologist,* 62:58–80.

WHITE, LESLIE, 1957, "How Morgan Came to Write Systems of Consanguinity and Affinity," *Papers of the Michigan Academy of Science, Arts, and Letters,* 42:257–268.

WILLIAM, THOMAS, 1967, *Field Methods in the Study of Culture.* New York: Holt, Rinehart and Winston.